The In[...]
Naval Revolt
of 1946

Percy S. Gourgey

Ex-Lieutenant RINVR, MBE, FRSA

Orient Longman

The publishers thank *The Times of India* Research
Department for permission to reproduce the
photographs in this volume,
including those on the cover.

ORIENT LONGMAN LIMITED

Registered Office :
3-6-272 Himayatnagar, Hyderabad 500 029 (A.P), India

Other Offices :
Bangalore/Bhopal/Bhubaneshwar/Calcutta/Chennai
Ernakulam/Guwahati/Hyderabad/Jaipur
Lucknow/Mumbai/New Delhi/Patna

© Orient Longman Limited 1996

First Published 1996
Reprinted 1998

ISBN 81 250 1136 6

Laser Typeset by
OSDATA
Himayatnagar
Hyderabad 500 029

Printed in India by
Indcom Press
West Mambalam
Chennai 600 033

Published by
Orient Longman Limited
160 Anna Salai
Chennai 600 002

Contents

Contents

Foreword

In the early weeks of 1946, I was privileged to be a member of the Parliamentary 'Goodwill' Mission to India. After a strenuous and exciting tour we reached England again on February 12, and a week later began the serious episode which Mr Gourgey so graphically narrates in the following pages.

While there is no connection between the two events, nevertheless my experience of the tense political atmosphere then prevailing in India enabled me to appreciate why the 'strike' or 'mutiny' of Indian naval ratings occurred.

Among innumerable interviews ranging from those with Gandhi, Nehru and Jinnah to humble villagers, I also met ex-members of the 'Indian National Army' composed, as the author mentions, of Indian prisoners-of-war in Japanese hands and led by Subhas Chandra Bose. They were obviously anxious and spiritually bewildered as they sought to analyse, and then convey to me, their motivation in first fighting with and for, and then against, the British. On my part, I confess to a certain embarrassment, for as a British citizen, and Member of Parliament, I had no sympathy with active or passive support for the Axis Powers and believed that the victory of Japanese forces in India would have been disastrous not merely to European but also to Indian and Asian democracy and freedom. Yet I realised that the action of those ex-prisoners who joined the INA did not issue from admiration for Japan, but from patriotic zeal for the independence of India. I too endorsed that purpose, although not the expedient unhappily accepted by Bose and his followers. This, indeed, was also the attitude of Gandhi and most of the Indian leaders, notwithstanding considerable evidence of contrary emotional admiration for Bose in many Indian quarters.

This psychological ambivalence appears in Mr Gourgey's record of the naval disturbance, even if its initial incidence at Bombay was due to resentment against slow demobilisation, inadequate pay, alleged contemptuous treatment and other human grievances. Such agitation, however, inevitably fanned the hot embers of nationalism so that economic, sociological and political elements fused (as they also did in the French and Russian revolutions) in the resultant flames. Moreover, hardship had frequently been attributed to alien authority in India, and I found a general assumption with many poor Indians that when 'Quit India' had been obeyed by the British, more rice would speedily follow.

No doubt, normally the relationship between British naval officers and Indian ratings had not been unfriendly, but apart from a continuously latent resentment against a preponderating British officer class, there were instances of racial oral humiliation, an example of which has been referred to by the author early in his record.

The flames flared and spread, to the angry alarm of the British authorities and to the discomfiture of Indian Congress leaders whose onerous task would have suffered gravely had the revolt continued. Those leaders recognised the poignancy of conflicting loyalties among the ratings, and for that matter among all Indian servicemen and civil servants, but confusion would have overwhelmed their efforts had the naval revolt expanded. To the British it was 'mutiny', even as the previous historic defiance by Indian leaders and their followers had been regarded as intolerable lawlessness if not treachery. To Indians, who sought liberation from British domination, it could be as much patriotic resentment as it was in the minds of Ulstermen in Northern Ireland at the prospect of absorption in a Catholic-dominated seceding Irish Government, or in the minds of the French *maquis* fighting against Nazi occupation of their country. One man's 'mutiny' is another man's 'loyalty'.

Even so, the Congress itself could not tolerate the sectional or local impulses that would nullify its responsible authority and bring about anarchic disintegration, even though it sympathised with its compatriots in their immediate grievance and their ultimate aspiration. This was but one component of the situation. Another was the perplexing dilemma attending the pursuit of Gandhian principles of *satyagraha* or non-violent resistance—a dilemma still haunting present Indian policy. In this connection the dialogue between ex-Lieut P.S. Gourgey and Punnu Khan has a moving significance, not least the contention of the latter that he and other would-be *satyagrahis* could not be held responsible for violent excesses by those who could not or would not observe the requisite moral and spiritual discipline. The report of the conversation in the context of disorder and violence may not be *verbatim* but in essence it is not only true but also illuminates a crucial moral issue beneath the external circumstances then prevailing.

I commend Mr Gourgey's record both for its historical and human value. It is one episode out of very many, but it contains much that illustrates the consummation of a massive political struggle, the immediate occasion for the over-flowing of human discontent and the interplay of the many forces that operate in a crisis of human behaviour. I am grateful that Mr Gourgey has asked me to write this 'Foreword', for while there may be some things to deplore in those distant years of prolonged striving for Indian freedom, yet I believe there is far more that heartens and inspires beyond the tribulation. Between the time I first met the author and the present time, India has become a free and sovereign State in equality with Britain in the Commonwealth and with all other nations. Her destiny, like her Navy, is in her own hands and those of us who played even a fragmentary part to achieve this can appreciate both the tragedy within the struggle and the majesty of the achievement.

by Lord Sorensen (formerly Reg W. Sorensen, MP)

Preface and Acknowledgements

In May and August 1995 respectively, the fiftieth anniversary of VE-Day and VJ-Day was marked by many celebrations and functions in those nations which played their part in the Second World War. A war in which over fifty million people were killed between 1939 and 1945 during the aggressive campaigns launched by Nazi Germany and imperialist Japan to achieve world domination.

It is worthy of note that India played a role in this War through the participation of the largest volunteer armed forces in the world—a fact that was recognised in the representation of these forces at victory parades held in London and elsewhere in 1945. It was also a momentous period in India's unique freedom struggle leading to independence from two centuries of British rule in August 1947. One dramatic event of the time was the famous 'Indian National Army' trials in Delhi in 1946. Another equally dramatic but not so well known event was the Royal Indian Navy 'mutiny' which took place in February 1946 when, within the space of one short week, the whole gamut of emotions experienced in the national liberation movement were manifested—fear, suspicion, jealousy, frustration and courage.

As a serving officer at the time, in the Royal Indian Naval Volunteer Reserve, I had the unique opportunity of witnessing at first hand the battle which took place in and around Bombay harbour. I was one of the officers trapped in the Central Communications Office just outside Castle Barracks, or HMIS *Dalhousie* to give it its official name, which was then the virtual headquarters of the Navy. This is therefore, essentially a personal account of the happenings which coincided with the visit of the British Cabinet Mission to India. The tense political situation which prevailed at that time was described by Jawaharlal Nehru as "a political earthquake of devastating intensity which might well sweep the entire country".

Acknowledgements are made to the following sources from which I gathered the necessary background information: the British Museum Library, the *Times of India* and other Indian newspapers filed in the Museum Hansard, i.e., the record of Parliamentary proceedings, Jane's Fighting Ships and the Royal United Services Institute for Defence Studies in London.

Percy S. Gourgey

1

A Feeling of Unrest

The ratings moved around in a slovenly fashion on the quarter-deck. Unshaven and unkempt in appearance, their caps at a rakish angle, they lounged around with their hands in their pockets. At the far end stood a small group of their divisional officers, anxiously conversing with each other, looking worried, brooding . . .

Instead of the usual smart, disciplined turn-out, this was the bewildering scene that greeted my eyes as I alighted from the car at 8.45 a.m. and walked to my office in Castle Barracks – the main shore establishment of the Royal Indian Navy in Bombay – on that cold, sunny morning of Tuesday, February 19, 1946. Stopping a Leading Seaman who was on my staff, I asked him why he was not at his post and in a sullen manner he replied: "Strike, sir!"

"Strike?" I echoed, "but that's impossible! There's no such thing as a *strike* in the armed forces: it's *mutiny*."

My way was barred by a messenger who had come from the Commanding Officer with an urgent summons to his office. Several other officers were already there and in a grim, strained voice, the CO said:

> This is it! For the first time in the history of the Navy, we have a mutiny on our hands. I've had direct orders from the Admiral that for the present no coercion is to be used against the ratings until further instructions. No interviews with the press should be granted. We don't know the cause or

the extent of the mutiny,[1] which the ratings call a 'strike', but we have to move carefully before taking any disciplinary action. Be at hand in case I have to call you again!

After the meeting with the CO, several of us went to the officers' mess to discuss the situation in an attempt to fathom the cause of recent similar happenings which we learnt had broken out in other establishments of the armed forces.

It was true that the country was in a state of great turmoil. The recent trials of the Indian National Army[2] had inflamed nationalists throughout the length and breadth of India.

Towards the end of the preceding month, a 'Subhas Bose Day' was organised during which the crowds in New Delhi ran amuck and attacked many officers. At a mass meeting on January 26 – barely three weeks earlier – Pandit Nehru had declared:

> Independence is not far off now, non-violence is the only rightful way . . . the only instrument which could give a slave country like India, as it stands at present, the strength of mass activity.

---

1.   Mutiny occurs in the armed forces when two or more men present the same grievance at the same time.

2.   The Indian National Army had been organised by the Indian National Congress leader,Subhas Chandra Bose,who in 1941 had escaped from house arrest in Calcutta and had gone over to the Axis Powers. After negotiations with the Japanese in 1943, he created, in Japanese-occupied Singapore, the nucleus of an army whose purpose was, he declared, to fight the British in India in cooperation with the Japanese, and later set up an independent Indian Government. For this purpose Bose recruited Indian prisoners-of-war held by the Japanese, who had then engaged in fighting against the British in Burma, under their own 'flag of independence' with the spirit of the Rani of Jhansi who, Bose recalled, was a famous national heroine of the 'Indian Mutiny' of 1857. At the end of the War, the Indian National Army leaders were captured and put on trial at the Red Fort in New Delhi. Speaking in the Council of State, General Auckinleck, War Member of the Viceroy's Executive Council and Commander-in-Chief of the Armed Forces in India, in reply to a resolution on the pending court-martial, declared: "Government policy had been to prove the principle that it was not open to a soldier to change his allegiance on account of his political opinions. But it was decided in view of the circumstances to extend mercy to those convicted of this offence; but to condone acts of gross brutality would be utterly wrong and most unfair to men who had suffered so cruelly at the hands of those who were to be tried." (Bose had disappeared under mysterious circumstances but it was later learnt that he died in an air crash near Bangkok. He was by then a legendary hero.)

Before returning to India, Vijayalakshmi Pandit, Nehru's sister, had said in New York that:

> events of the past four or five years have created a militant mood amongst the people of India . . . we hope that the American people could in some way support the Indian cause. With such nations as Australia and New Zealand coming out strongly for colonial independence, the world's mood is such that we have more of a chance to take our freedom. Let us work so that independence will be an accomplished fact by January 1947.

At the time, a British parliamentary delegation was touring India and its leading member, Mr R. W. Sorensen, MP, had said:

> I want India to be a great India, a splendid India. The greatness not to be measured by territory, by numbers or by military achievements but measured by moral, social and democratic qualities. I want the two countries, Britain and India, to be friends and there can be no true and durable friendship save on the basis of mutual respect. I pray that the day will come when the hand of friendship shall be stretched out from India to England and from England to India. From both points of view, I believe it must be accepted that British rule must end. The only question is how this can be effected. We had some conversation on this and its bearing on the issue of Pakistan.

Other members of the delegation were Mr G. Nicholson and Lord Chorley who said:

> Everyone in England is anxious to do the right thing by India and . . . they are anxious to be well-informed about Indian affairs. Every section of the British public is anxious that India should be mistress of her own destiny as soon as possible.

Indian Congress leaders such as Mahatma Gandhi, Pandit Nehru, Sardar Vallabhai Patel and Maulana Abul Kalam Azad, Congress President at the time, had been released from a three-year imprison-ment term in June 1945. The Viceroy, Lord Wavell, shortly afterwards convened a Conference of Indian leaders to resolve the constitutional stalemate in India: it had resulted in an abortive attempt at revolution made after the historic 'Quit India' Resolution of August 8, 1942 passed by the All India Congress Committee in Bombay where, as a journalist, I was present. The All India Muslim League had, after VJ-Day in August 1945, resumed its agitation for Pakistan under the leadership of Mohamad Ali Jinnah (who founded the Dominion of Pakistan two years later).

3

Nevertheless, it was amazing to see how both the Congress and the Muslim League were prepared to sink their differences in order to champion the cause of the aggrieved Royal Indian Navy ratings. The 'iron man' of the Indian National Congress, Sardar Vallabhai Patel, later to become India's Deputy Prime Minister, had declared at the outbreak of the mutiny that:

> those who seek to uphold imperialism and perpetuate inequalities can ill-afford to talk of prestige, much less of vindicating it, in the present awakening and consequent determined opposition of which the recent events are convincing evidence. *Being a witness to the recent happenings in Bombay, I can say nothing like it has happened within this generation.* The destruction of property was wantonly thoughtless. There is no doubt that what happened was a direct outcome of the War that has only officially closed and an echo of what is happening in the West (and elsewhere: Indonesia, Greece, Palestine, Persia, etc.). The inequality, which still seems to reign supreme and which it is hoped would die out, was galling for the Indian ratings and resentment of the distinctions between Europeans and Indians made them impatient to the point of hurting, what was bound to be, a futile defiance on the part of an ill-armed few against overwhelming odds, fully armed.

Dwelling on the reaction of the people, Mr Patel went on to say:

> The populace, whose sympathy has always been with the fighters against imperialism, readily joined hands and brushed aside the wise counsels of leaders who love liberty no less than they . . .

Reports had appeared that in the House of Commons at Westminster, Mr Attlee was preparing the historic statement that he was shortly to make on the constitutional measures leading to self-government in India. He was British Prime Minister at the time.

After our conversations and references to various newspapers in the mess library, we returned to our duties full of foreboding. We did not have long to wait. Official information had just come through of the incidents which had occurred on the previous day (Monday, February 18).

2

Day One of the Revolt

All ratings numbering about a thousand, with the exception of Chief Petty Officers and Petty Officers, of HMIS *Talwar*, the Royal Indian Navy School of Signals at Colaba in South Bombay, had refused to report for duty. They had also begun a hunger strike.

A chain of events had led to this state of affairs. The release of the Indian leaders in June 1945, their negotiations with the Viceroy (Lord Wavell), the end of the War against Japan, the INA trials, and a small but ineffective mutiny in the Royal Indian Air Force earlier that year had resulted in a mounting fever of excitement affecting the whole political climate.

Nationalist feelings were running high in the Armed Forces, and the Navy was no exception. At HMIS *Talwar*, the ratings serving in the signals school were probably the most literate and intelligent in the entire Navy. Some of them had taken to writing on the walls of the establishment,political slogans like: *Quit India, Down with British Raj, Victory to Gandhi and Nehru*. The authorities were not immediately able to identify the ringleaders, who had called for a 'slow down' strike among their fellow-ratings.

The Commanding Officer of *Talwar*, tall, bearded, powerfully-built Commander F.W. King, incensed by the slogan-writing, the go-slow methods and certain other acts of indiscipline, had ordered the personnel in the Regulating Office to show proper marks of respect and proceed immediately with their duties. When they did not 'jump to it', he reportedly bellowed: "Hurry, you sons of coolies and bitches!" Word went round the establishment like wild-fire and work ceased as if by magic. Ratings thronged to the Regulating Office yelling "Quit India"!

With considerable difficulty, and aided by his junior officers, Commander King made his way through the menacing crowd of ratings and went straight to his office. He quickly got into contact with the Flag Officer, Bombay (FOB), Rear-Admiral Rattray, reporting the incidents. This report was flashed to Vice-Admiral Godfrey, Flag Officer Commanding, Royal Indian Navy (FOCRIN) at Naval Headquarters in New Delhi.

Back at *Talwar*, the ringleaders, amongst whom was Leading Signalman Punnu Khan – later to play a prominent part – formed a Strike Committee and seized control of the signals instruments. They radioed messages to all naval establishments in India, and also to RIN ships at sea, urging all hands to strike. Many establishments picking up these signals were in and around Bombay, Karachi and Cochin on the western coast and in Calcutta, Chittagong, Vizagapatam and Madras on the eastern coast.

The Communications ratings who manned the signals immediately passed on the word to their fellow-ratings. Strike Committees were formed in all establishments and, following the example of *Talwar*, they presented petitions to their Commanding Officers setting forth their grievances. These were immediately reported to Staff Officers and finally channelled through to NHQ in New Delhi. The ratings demanded quicker demobilisation and resettlement, revision of pay and allowances, better Indian food and speedier Indianisation of the officer cadres of the Navy.

The process of demobilisation seemed unnecessarily slow. The majority of the thousands of ratings, who had volunteered for the duration of the hostilities only, were eager to get back to 'civvy street' and return to their homes and families, in faraway towns and villages.[1] Moreover, competition for civilian jobs had increased every month since the end of the War. But red tape, bureaucracy, and the attitude of senior staff officers at Naval Headquarters (most of them British) who behaved like "tin gods and *burrah sahibs*", made for frustrating and irritating delays.

---

1. By then two million in Britain's Armed Forces had already been demobilised.

Again, with the cost of living becoming inflationary, pay and allowances were inadequate, particularly when the ratings sent to their poverty-stricken homes a fairly large proportion of their pay. At the best of times it compared unfavourably with the rates of pay received by personnel of the Royal Navy in India doing similar jobs, and this tended to exacerbate the situation.

The inferior quality of food received by the Indian ratings formed the subject of another grievance. Not too much imagination or ingenuity needed to be exercised to visualise the kind of food that would be appreciated by Indian ratings.

But what possibly hurt nationalist feelings most was the proposal that was being aired at the time, to draft about four hundred Royal Navy officers for service with the Royal Indian Navy. Why not recruit Indian officers instead? This was the question often asked and to which no satisfactory reply was given. If the Indian Navy of the future was going to serve an India in complete control of her own destiny, surely now was the time to train Indians for this task. After all, during the War India had had the largest *volunteer* army in the world, perhaps in history, numbering about two million, and she was therefore not lacking in suitable personnel. (Or was the idea to proceed with Indianisation so slowly, that only after another thirty years would an Indian General emerge on the scene—as was Nehru's scornful comment in his autobiography!)

Thus ran the thoughts and arguments of nationalist-minded Indians.

The Central Communications Office outside Castle Barracks was, in the normal course of affairs, a hive of activity. It received, de-coded and re-routed signals of all kinds from all over India, shore establishments, coastal forces, and ships in the Indian Ocean. When signals of the strike first came through, officers and ratings alike were stunned. This was unprecedented and incredible!

Had *Talwar* taken leave of its senses? What could have gone wrong? It was decided to send two Indian officers at once to *Talwar* to make a personal check and report.

Sure enough, on their return an hour later they confirmed that *Talwar* had gone on strike. Ratings were in complete control. Commander King was in his quarters, and outwardly there was a deceptive calm. No violence had occurred in the establishment. Normal routine was hardly disrupted. The only difference was that the *Talwar* Strike Committee was in charge.

What was to be done now in the CCO? It was decided to relay all messages received to NHQ (I) in Delhi, and await further instructions. Rear-Admiral Rattray, Flag Officer, Bombay was already informed of developments and was in touch with Vice-Admiral Godfrey, Flag Officer Commanding, Royal Indian Navy in Delhi.

But it seemed that initially confusion and doubt reigned. No proper official assessment of the situation was made. The scope and extent of the mutiny – for that was what it was seen to be right from the start – was not fully recognised. Authority was loath to believe that such a thing could happen in the *Navy*. Utterly respectable, quietly efficient, proud of its traditions, enjoying a high status, admired and loved by the public, how *could* anything go wrong? Despite its small size, had it not rendered fine service during the War? Providing escort vessels for convoys, minesweeping, patrolling India's coastline which was thousands of miles long, engaging the enemy in the Bay of Bengal, the Arabian Sea, and off the Arakan Coast, organising hit-and-run raids by coastal vessels in the Burmese *chaungs* (creeks), and attacking the Japanese-occupied Andaman and Nicobar Islands? Did not a small Indian sloop sink a Japanese cruiser off India's west coast in 1942? Its CO, Lieutenant-Commander Wilson, had been decorated with the DSO and a public reception had been held for him and his crew in Bombay, after a march through streets lined with cheering crowds. It had developed from small beginnings at the outbreak of the War to its present strength, where it could compare favourably with some of the other Commonwealth and Allied navies.

Thus disaffection and mutiny were unthinkable!

In the meantime, the officers and ratings comprising the staff of the CCO were taking stock. A small supply of arms was stored there over which a double guard was mounted. Late on Monday evening, news of the mutiny had already spread amongst all the personnel of Castle Barracks. Leave was cancelled, the guard everywhere was strengthened and a security check was made of all incoming ratings reporting for draft as the main Drafting Office was in Castle Barracks.

The ratings themselves remained in their quarters trying to appraise the situation. The few who had earlier got wind of the mutiny were busy organising the Strike Committee, arguing, persuading, coaxing and bullying others into compliance. Many doubted the wisdom of taking part in the mutiny or, indeed, of the very staging of it. Years of training and discipline had so conditioned their reflexes that disobeying the orders of their superiors was difficult if not impossible.

No doubt the confusion that prevailed at NHQ (I) was reflected in other parts of the Service too. Many believed that the legitimate grievances, as enumerated in the *Talwar* signals, could be redressed through normal channels. They believed that though this would take time, it was by far the best way. They doubtless also had misgivings about the disciplinary action that would surely follow. Irresponsible action near the termination of their service might prove too costly, resulting in the possible loss of pension, gratuity and other benefits. A considerable proportion, however, felt that only drastic action like a mutiny could yield effective results.

As night fell and the Officer-on-Watch went on his rounds, an air of expectancy hung about the Barracks. The OOW received sharp answers to his customary questions to the ratings about their welfare. They did not respond readily nor did they spring to attention on hearing the piping that signalled the arrival of the Officer on his rounds through the Barracks. A certain tension·was already evident, and signs of frayed nerves were visible. As 'Lights Out' was sounded, an uneasy calm descended over the whole establishment. In Bombay itself little was foreseen that night of the hectic events that would follow in the next few days.

3
Day Two

By now news of the mutiny had spread to all parts of India through newspapers and All India Radio. The civilian populace of Bombay tended to discount rumours of various incidents, believing that the authorities would have the situation well under control. This was a not unexpected reaction resulting from experience gained during periods of Hindu-Muslim communal rioting. It was generally found that rumours always tended to exacerbate the situation, inflame tempers and possibly lead to violence and bloodshed. The more responsible elements amongst the public helped to exercise a restraining influence by their ready inclination to scotch these rumours on the spot. Hence 'business as usual' was the order of the day and this usually produced a calming effect.

Nevertheless, on the second day of the mutiny events were moving fast in the naval shore establishments and in ships at sea.

In Castle Barracks, where all officers were at their posts awaiting further instructions from their CO,[1] normal routine was suspended. Although discipline had not entirely broken down, the ratings refused to carry out their daily duties and it was thought best not to attempt coercion. News was rapidly coming through of ratings assuming control of various ships in and around Bombay harbour.

On one frigate – a larger RIN vessel – the entire Strike Committee went to the CO to ask him to confine himself and his brother-officers

---

10   1.   Captain H.R. Inigo-Jones, RIN.

to the ward room. It was futile for the CO to refuse as no other ratings would obey his orders. Any attempt at violent resistance could result in disaster as the first place the Strike Committee took control of was the ship's armoury. This followed on the report of the strike which was first received by the ratings manning the ship's signals system, which included morse, wireless telegraphy or semaphore. In fact, the Communications ratings usually formed the leadership of the Strike Committee, according to the pattern set in *Talwar*.

The Central Strike Committee in *Talwar* issued a stream of instructions to Strike Committees in all ships and establishments to maintain good order and discipline once they assumed control, to keep violence down to a minimum and to refrain from causing injury or insult to officers who had handed over authority.

On many ships the generally sound discipline that had previously obtained led to a quiet handing over of authority. The good sense and, often, friendship between officers and ratings helped to reduce the number of incidents on ships. In any case, those ratings who might have disobeyed the orders of the Strike Committee leaders were usually in a hopeless minority or were quickly deprived of possible control of the ship's armoury. Thus, where there was resistance to the Strike Committee's orders, officers and loyal ratings were quickly overpowered.

Indian officers on ships and also in shore establishments were in a particular dilemma. For though it was true that their first loyalty lay to the Crown, they nevertheless felt a special sympathy for the cause of the ratings who, rightly or wrongly, believed their mutiny was justified. In most cases the Indian officers acted as mediators between the Strike Committee, which instinctively turned to them, and the British Commanding Officers of ships and establishments, wherever assumption of control was initially sought by peaceful methods. As a result, casualty figures were surprisingly low for a mutiny which had assumed countrywide proportions. While this was generally true of the Navy as such, it was certainly not the case among the civilian populace and cities of India where, as Sardar Patel declared, "the destruction of property was wantonly thoughtless".

In Castle Barracks the ratings showed increasing restlessness and eventually in the late afternoon a number of them, led by members of the Strike Committee, declared their intention of proceeding ashore to join the others in *Talwar*. On receiving the nominal consent of their

Divisional Officers – hardly necessary, yet so strong was their trained sense of discipline! – they marched out of the Barracks in a more or less orderly fashion. They joined up with other groups of ratings from other shore establishments and together marched through the streets of Bombay on their way to *Talwar*, where a mass meeting of ratings was to be addressed by leaders of the Central Strike Committee including Leading Signalman Punnu Khan.

They had to pass through the chief business centre in Hornby Road, (now Mahatma Gandhi Road) in the Fort area of Bombay. Some provocative comments by passers-by, coupled with a current of excitement generated by thousands of their comrades from sloops and minesweepers coming together and shouting slogans such as *Mahatma Gandhi-ki Jai* (Long live Gandhi) and *Inquilab Zindabad* (Victory to the Revolution) roused passions to fever pitch—and suddenly, it was hell let loose!

They ran wild, singling out Britons for attack, stopping buses and private cars and hauling both British and Indian drivers of Service vehicles from their seats. Civilians were forced to remove ties and sun topees – seen as symbols of alien dress smacking of alien rule – and these were burned in a huge bonfire at Flora Fountain, the very heart of Bombay's main banking and insurance centre.

I saw an RN Petty Officer caught in the crowd forced to remove his cap which was slung into the bonfire. The *goonda* or hooligan elements of Bombay's underworld took advantage of the situation and joined in the rioting. A huge mob converged on to Flora Fountain to hear a harangue given by one of the leaders of the march.

Raising his voice above the clamour he thundered: "Down with the hated foreign ruler! The day of our independence is very near. If they don't give us the sweet fruit of freedom dangled before us we shall snatch it from their grasp . . . " Hardly had he uttered these words when his voice was drowned in a shrill crescendo of police whistles and the thud of truncheons and *lathis*.

The crowd ran helter-skelter before this charge, many seeking refuge in shops and doorways, only to be hurriedly turned away by nervous shopkeepers who pulled down steel shutters and locked themselves inside.

Pandemonium broke loose as the mounted police emerged on the scene to be greeted by a hail of stones, garbage and abuse. Many ratings escaped through side-streets and narrow lanes to join up into gangs further away and advance menacingly on the police. The familiar weapons of street rioting, seen before in communal rioting, were all brought into play. One particularly vicious weapon was that of a peculiar way of slinging soda-water bottles, grabbed from nearby restaurants, at a terrific speed to land thirty yards away and explode with the force of a hand grenade, showering dangerous splinters all around.

Another was setting caps or hats alight to send them sailing through the air, burning anyone and anything on which they landed.

Sporadic rioting continued for a couple of hours until dusk fell – about 7.00 p.m. – by which time police reinforcements were rushed up, arresting many rioters and driving them away in police vans. All local jails that night were filled to bursting point. Outside each a crowd gathered, chanting nationalist slogans and demanding the release of the inmates.

Bombay went to bed that night with revolution in the air, rioting, looting and acts of violence having broken out in all parts of the city. Added numbers of patrol cars equipped with radio sets were on the streets to deter would-be rioters. Troop reinforcements were brought up from Poona but their turn for action came only the next day.

4

Day Three

Reporting for duty at 8.30 a.m., an astonishing scene presented itself as I walked up the long road leading to Castle Barracks. Contingents of the Indian and British Army, including battalions of the 18th Mahrattas and Leicestershires used in other parts of Bombay as well, were drawn up near the gates and, under the orders of a British captain, had assumed a firing position. Large numbers of ratings were crouching before them in disorderly array, yelling insults and curses and throwing stones, bottles and anything they could lay their hands on.

"How do you come to be here? What has happened?" I queried a subedar-major.

"We were ordered to proceed here in the early hours of this morning, sir," he replied. "During the night the situation in the Barracks deteriorated rapidly; the ratings became noisy and their leaders allowed them to break into the armoury, take the rifles and fire some rounds into the air. It was feared they might break out into the city."

"I suppose it's fortunate they don't have their arms with them just now," I rejoined. "Their leaders must have regained control of the rifles and ammunition."

The ratings were now approaching dangerously close, the troops were ordered to be prepared to open fire. Suddenly a hail of stones, bottles and tins fell in a shower over them and at their feet. The captain muttered to his men: "When I give the order to fire, fire a warning volley into the air."

Another shower of stones and bottles.

"*Ek* round, fire!" shouted the captian.

The first volley in the mutiny rang out. The crowds of ratings melted into the walls and doorways of the wartime hutments and canteens on either side of the road. A few minutes later they re-emerged. I saw a rating fifteen yards away take aim and sling a large stone which struck the subedar-major I had spoken to earlier. As blood flowed from the side of his face, very deliberately he drew his revolver and pulled back the safety-catch. As he took aim, I brought my hand sharply down on his wrist and deflected the shot.

"What are you doing?" I yelled. "Can't you see he is unarmed, a little mad? Don't you realise what could happen if you hit him?"

The captain supported my action, though he himself had now been struck by a stone and was slightly injured. He ordered the subedar to return to the lorries which had brought up the troops.

The more responsible leaders among the ratings saw that only harm could come to them if they persisted in challenging the troops, and firmly they ordered their followers to return down the road and back through the gates of Castle Barracks.

As it was now impossible to enter the Barracks I went a few minutes' walk away to the RIN Staff Offices in Mint Road.

Grim reports were pouring in now of the speedily worsening situation all over the country.

At the naval base in Calcutta, HMIS *Hooghly*, the ratings mutinied as soon as they had signals of the outbreak in Bombay. Even more than in Bombay, in Calcutta the political atmosphere was the cause of immediate tension. For Calcutta, the capital city of Bengal, and second largest city of the British Commonwealth and Empire at the time, was always distinguished for its acute political consciousness, providing many of the famous leaders of the Indian freedom movement. Indeed, was it not the home for many years of one of India's greatest revolutionary leaders and founder of the INA, Netaji Subhas Chandra Bose? Did not the patriot and greatest Indian *litterateur* of modern times, Rabindranath Tagore, live and work there and establish near the city, his famous university at Santiniketan? Both in the early years of this century and on the threshold of independence a year later, Calcutta was the heart of the nationalist movement.

In Karachi, Indian ratings on board HMIS *Hindustan* retaliated with two naval guns against fire opened by the military police. The Keamari naval area was cordoned off from the city by British soldiers armed with tommy-guns. In the shore establishments of HMIS *Chamak*, *Himalaya* (the RIN gunnery school), and *Bahadur* (the Boys' Training Ship), one thousand five hundred ratings had joined the mutiny earlier in the day.

The *Hindustan* was due to sail, but her departure had to be postponed owing to twelve ratings, including the wireless operator, going on strike. They alleged that the ship's captain and executive officer had insulted them and they put forward a set of grievances similar to that of *Talwar*.

In HMIS *India* at Naval Headquarters in New Delhi, about eighty naval ratings, mainly telegraphists and signalmen, refused to continue work. Similar reports were coming in from Cochin and from HMIS *Adyar* in Madras—the latter I knew well having been stationed there during the War.

Late on Wednesday afternoon, the ratings in Castle Barracks had withdrawn completely behind the walls and from a distance could be seen keeping watch from its ramparts.

A number of officers who had duties inside Castle Barracks decided to return to the CCO just outside the Barracks. This had been constantly manned by a few officers as well as ratings who had not joined the mutineers. While in the CCO, we heard sounds of shouting and rushing feet outside. Going out to investigate we learnt that some ratings had been arrested for disobeying an order to return to their ships, and as they were being removed in lorries from Castle Barracks under the guard of troops, about fifty ratings rushed out of the Barracks after them, shouting slogans and engaging in a demonstration.

A confused situation had developed in Castle Barracks. For although the Strike Committee was in control, continuous contact, largely telephonic, was maintained not only with mutineers in other establishments but also with RIN headquarters nearby in Mint Road. The Strike Committee sought to keep acts of violence and indiscipline to a minimum fearing the consequences of not doing so, and also as a result of the apparent reluctance of Congress leaders to support them. But it was not anticipated that when troops came to remove

16

some of the mutineers, the reaction of their fellows would be so fierce.

As the lorries sped away, ratings rushed down the road. At the end of the road, when they were outside the gates of Castle Barracks, units of the 18th Mahrattas, a famous battle-scarred Indian infantry regiment, quickly drew up across the road blocking all entrance or exit. It was a discreet move on the part of the authorities to use Indian troops at this juncture, as they would be less likely than British troops to cause provocation and resentment among the mutinying sailors. Nevertheless, the mere sight of the military – "inferior pongos!" – caused anger. This I was to ascertain somewhat later.

As we knew personally a number of the ratings rushing past, I suggested to my brother-officers that we form a kind of cordon between them and the troops at the end of the road, to prevent as far as possible any kind of contact which would result in violence and bloodshed. Immediately about a dozen of us pelted for the gates just ahead of the ratings running fast at our heels.

On reaching the gates, we instantly about-turned and formed a cordon in front of the troops stretching right across the road. Not a moment too soon! The first ratings caught up with us and we pushed them back. Almost instinctively, we held hands forming a human barrier across the road in much the same way that police lining the route of a procession prevent the crowds from surging forward. This was rather different as behind us the troops stood firm with bayonets fixed and in front of us was a storming, heaving mass of roaring, angry ratings. We cursed, coaxed, exhorted and bullied our men.

"Go back, go back!" we yelled. Both naval officers and men recognised each other and the old sense of comradeship and mutual respect helped exercise a certain restraining influence for a few precious moments.

A Petty Officer from my office began speaking to me:

"Get those troops out of the way, sir."

"I can't," I retorted, "they're not under my command, and they have their job to do."

"Listen, sir!" he shouted, eyes blazing, "we have only a few minutes now. I don't care how, but those troops must be removed. They are like a red rag to a bull to our fellows! For have we not been told that the Navy is the senior service? Those of us in the Barracks have now taken Sten guns, rifles, bayonets and revolvers from the armoury and we have plenty of ammunition. They can see us," he added, pointing to the glare of lights streaming from the surrounding buildings. "If we don't succeed in removing the troops, at least from their sight," he went on, "they will open fire, even if it means hitting us. This was planned earlier in the evening!"

Cold fear gripped my heart. Even more than the time during the War when our little ships were shelled by Japanese coastal batteries in Ramree Island off the Arakan Coast in Burma. For this was something personal. We had worked with and had come to know these men in the course of our routine duties in the Barracks. But anything could happen now, with the rising anger of these men at what they regarded as the stupid injustice of the authorities.

I looked around and saw that we were hemmed in from all sides, trapped between the ratings and the troops and the high walls of the buildings on either side of the road. No chance now of making a break for it! Driven by sheer desperation — for I was still a sub-lieutenant at twenty-two — I turned to the tall English major in command of the troops.

"Can't you move them out," I bellowed above the din.

"Sorry, old man," he yelled back. "I have the orders of the Commander-in-Chief, General Auckinleck, to see that the ratings don't break out into the city!"

I felt beads of sweat on my brow as we were being pushed back towards the glistening bayonets held so firmly by the unyielding Mahrattas. We were now only a few inches away.

"Look here!" I roared at the major, "you are the man on the spot and you have to make your own decisions now. We know these ratings and they ask only that the troops be moved out of sight. Order them to withdraw to either side of the road!"

The pressure was now at bursting point.

Two other officers joined me in yelling at the major. At the cost of breaking the cordon we caught hold of him and one drew his revolver from its socket. Suddenly his mind was made up.

"To hell with a damned court-martial," he screamed and commanded his men to fall back.

As the troops withdrew, the relief was instantaneous. The ratings cheered and for their part fell back.

Tension momentarily disappeared. Everyone relaxed for a little while. Nevertheless, the ratings were still discontented as they knew the troops had only drawn aside. They wanted them to leave if only as a gesture of confidence by the authorities in the sense of responsibility shown by them so far. For the mutineers could easily have destroyed much valuable naval equipment in ships and establishments. But on the sound advice of their leaders, they had not done so. By their conduct they wanted to demonstrate the genuineness of their grievances, which they felt were substantial and called for early redress.

However, no withdrawal of the troops was achieved. Or for that matter was possible, in view of the C-in-C's personal orders on containment of the ratings in their Barracks. The situation began to assume an ugly aspect all over again. Mutterings of discontent turned to shouts. The mutineers, who a few minutes ago had stood round quietly, became restless. Those farther down the road demanded to know what was happening.

They started to push forward. Those in front threw challenging looks at our small band of officers. They stood shoulder to shoulder and began to march steadily towards us. Their eyes bloodshot with fatigue and tension, they stormed and shouted. The troops looked attentively at the major in charge, expecting any moment the order to return to their previous positions across the road at the gates.

Tension mounted rapidly. Any minute now there would be a renewed attempt by the ratings to rush the gates, this time regardless of the consequences.

Suddenly from behind us a figure emerged from the dark, blowing sharp blasts on a whistle attached by a lanyard round his neck. Straining our eyes we discerned Leading Signalman Punnu Khan, an important member of the Central Strike Committee at *Talwar*.

We made way for him. He stood in front of the surging mass of mutineers, raised his arms above his head to bring them to a halt, and speaking in hoarse tones began to address them.

"Return to the Barracks," he said with a note of command in his voice. "We have begun negotiations with senior officers on the Admiral's staff. We have also approached Congress leaders, including Sardar Vallabhai Patel. He has promised us all support in our demands, but he has asked us to behave with discipline."

His words produced an instant effect. Such was the confidence he inspired that the crowds of ratings before him melted away. They walked back to their Barracks, talking cheerfully amongst themselves.

It was over! All of us sighed with relief. We returned to the CCO, Punnu Khan giving us information about the position in *Talwar* and in other shore establishments round Bombay, with which we had had no contact for the past twenty-four hours.

We relaxed in the small ward-room at the CCO and Punnu Khan went on to Castle Barracks to talk to the strike leaders. Somewhat later we received a signal that the Admiral (Flag Officer, Bombay) who had heard of the evening's incidents while at the Head Office in Mint Road, was coming to us on a tour of inspection in order to acquaint himself personally with all the details.

While we were reporting to him, suddenly in the doorway in some inexplicable manner appeared Punnu Khan—unless commanded by an officer, no rating could appear in the ward-room. On catching sight of the Admiral, he jumped smartly to attention, as did his followers behind him. Turning to him, the Admiral queried rather curtly:

"What's all the trouble about? Why did the ratings try to break out when negotiations are proceeding?"

"They were becoming impatient, sir," he retorted. And, as if to show to his followers that he was now talking to the Admiral on a basis of equality, he struck an indifferent attitude and leaned against the doorway. For us all it proved an embarrassing moment indeed! Perhaps it was a sign of the times that a rating could speak thus to an Admiral! Doubtless Punnu Khan wanted it to seem so, particularly since some of his followers were watching closely.

The Admiral quickly sized up the situation, turned and addressed a few words to us, and said to Punnu Khan: "Tell the members of your Committee to report to me for a meeting tomorrow," and left the CCO.

Thus, tact succeeded in maintaining dignity and order!

It was about 10.00 p.m. and many of us made to go home after an exhausting day. A skeleton staff remained for the night at the CCO. I was fortunate in being able to go home. But the day's events, the orgy of violence in some cities, had made a tremendous impact on me and until I had matters sorted out in my mind, even if only to a certain extent, I knew I would not be able to rest. Quickly making up my mind, I turned to Punnu Khan and asked him to accompany me with one of his followers, Telegraphist R. Singh, to a naval officers' club further away in the town. As it was late, I knew there would be hardly any other officers there who would object—especially at a time like this. And for my own personal information I wanted to talk to Punnu Khan about certain aspects of the situation.

Double deck tram set on fire on the night of 21.2.1946.
Courtesy: *The Times of India*, Research Department

Rowdyism by public crowds on the roads making bonfires of wood piles, broken from telephone boxes, shops, doors, etc. on Thursday morning. Courtesy: *The Times of India*, Research Department

Bonfire opposite Bazar Gate Post Office.
Courtesy: *The Times of India*, Research Department

The procession of RIN (Royal Indian Navy)
demonstrators in Bombay, who, armed with various
weapons, created a wave of terror in the Fort area on
Tuesday morning. The demonstration was in sympathy
with the "strike" of ratings of HMIS Talwar (published
in *The Times of India* 20.2.1946).
Courtesy: *The Times of India*, Research Department

Ratings of the RIN on strike in Bombay, who failed to
return to their ships and establishments by the specific
time on Wednesday afternoon were rounded up by the
military. Picture shows a rating who had not complied
with the order being led away by an escort (published in
The Times of India 21.2.1946).
Courtesy: *The Times of India*, Research Department

5

Non-Violence and Nationalism

At the Club, I went to the Officer's Mess which, fortunately, was empty. Settling myself in a comfortable arm-chair in the far corner and motioning Punnu Khan and his friend, Singh, to chairs opposite, I requested the steward to bring some drinks. He looked startled, but nevertheless complied.

"What do you hope to achieve by all this?" I asked Punnu Khan and Singh. "And how does politics come into it?"

"To put it in a nutshell, sir," said Punnu Khan, "we want the authorities to note and deal with our grievances. For many months, perhaps for two or three years, our grievances have been accumulating and really nothing has been done to deal with them to our satisfaction. In accordance with the regulations, we have, as individuals, made repeated complaints to our divisional officers and through them, to our commanding officers, but no action has been taken. They said they would look into our complaints, they have written many letters, asked us further questions, but no concrete results have yet been achieved."

"Take my case," interjected Singh eagerly. "I have my home and family in a village near Lahore in the Punjab. Last year there were floods in the area after an unusually heavy monsoon. My family including my wife and two children, with her aged father and mother, suffered greatly because our small patch of land was affected. Our crops were destroyed, our two cows drowned, our little house and belongings very badly damaged. My family members were evacuated by the authorities to a nearby village about a hundred miles away." He paused to take a puff at the cigarette I had offered him earlier, and continued: "They know nobody there, they get little to eat and they are living in one small room in a very large house where the authorities have placed fifty other families, who are living in the same way. My wife has written me many letters begging me to come home, complaining about the shortage of food for the family, and bad living conditions. In her last letter, she said her aged father had fallen ill and her mother was too old to be of much help to him. She needs me desperately. I have asked for one month's leave on compassionate grounds but it has been refused. The CO points to the regulations and says I have already taken one month's leave in the year. That is true, but it was shortly before the monsoons and the disaster which befell the family. What can I do?" he cried, throwing up his hands in despair.

Turning to Punnu Khan, I remarked, "I don't understand. If his CO has written letters to the local authorities, how is it nothing has been done so far?"

"I come from the same district," rejoined Punnu Khan. "In my case, my family are tenant-farmers, and they are too poor and too heavily in debt to pay their rent. The *zamindar* has threatened them with eviction, but they have nowhere to go. You can write a hundred letters to the SDO (sub-divisional officer) of the area, but he has a thousand problems, and it is often too late before he can deal with a special individual case. That is why we want leave so desperately, at least to try and settle our problems personally. For me there has also been delay in getting some back pay and allowances to help my family," he added resentfully. "I am due to be 'demobbed' in eight months' time. The War is over. If the Navy will release me, I am prepared to go tomorrow. Thousands of other ratings all over India are in a similar predicament," he observed, looking very distressed.

There was deep silence. I took a long sip at my drink.

"Why did you mutiny, and how did you come to do it in this way?" I persisted.

Giving me a hard look, Khan replied: "I told you, thousands of ratings have similar problems. Some time ago we in *Talwar* became absolutely fed up and decided something drastic must be done to shake the authorities. But we did not know where to begin, or how to organise ourselves. And then someone had an idea. Some of our friends got in touch with members of the Congress and other nationalists amongst the civilians. They told us all our troubles were due to foreign rule and until the British Raj was sent back to Britain, there would be no proper solution. They said ninety per cent of four hundred million Indians live in villages like our families and suffer from poverty, ignorance and illness. Only Indian leaders like Gandhi and Nehru, who have a deep understanding of the problems of their poor brothers and sisters, can lead the people out of their suffering and poverty.

"They suggested plans for a mass strike. The authorities may call it 'mutiny',"he added significantly, "but we understand mutiny to be the violent and bloody overthrow of the officers commanding us. On the other hand, our original intention was, and still is, to have a mass sit-down strike in all ships and establishments, until the authorities take sincere, concrete steps to settle our grievances. But we want this strike to be peaceful," he stressed. "If we can achieve our aims peacefully," he went on, "why should we want any harm to come to our superior officers?"

"But," I pointed out, "things have taken a violent turn. And not only in the Navy. Civilian riots have broken out all over India."

"We can't take responsibility for that," he broke in impatiently. "Who can blame the civilians if they show sympathy for *our* suffering, which is also *their* suffering, because we are all like brothers," he exclaimed enthusiastically. "Our common suffering unites us. Suffering gives the power to perceive and to understand. Mahatma Gandhi has said: 'My aim is to wipe every tear from every eye.' If he wants to remove pain and misery, then we who suffer, must we not follow him?"

The logic of his argument was irrefutable, though I pondered the wisdom of his action, especially as the Congress Working Committee had not yet displayed complete and unequivocal support for the mutiny. Nevertheless, Punnu Khan's fervent belief in the leadership of Mahatma Gandhi impressed me deeply. I recalled that on a former occasion, as a journalist I was similarly impressed by the emotions displayed by the audience on seeing and hearing Gandhiji. This occasion was the historic session of the All India Congress Committee in August 1942 at Gowalia Tank, Bombay when the revolutionary 'Quit India' resolution was passed, followed by three years' imprisonment for Gandhi, Nehru, Rajendra Prasad, Patel, Azad and other

Congress leaders. At this session, Congressmen gave vent to wild enthusiasm chanting "we are free, we are free!" and pinning on their shirts small paper flags bearing the likeness of Mahatma Gandhi.

I was still further intrigued by the emphasis Khan laid on the non-violent and nationalist aspirations of the leaders of the mutiny. Though I had some knowledge of the philosophy underlying Indian non-violence and nationalism, I probed further:

"If the mutineers are engaged in a sit-down strike of the kind you indicated," I enquired, "how could you expect the authorities not to resort to force ultimately to stop it?"

"We can only hope they won't," he answered. (I recalled an earlier statement of Gandhi's that he himself was an incurable optimist.)

Gourgey: But supposing they do! What then?

Khan: If we are true *satyagrahis* (believers in truth and non-violence) we shall still not resist them physically.

Gourgey: Aha! So you can be called passive resisters!

Khan: (brusquely) I don't like the word 'passive'. It gives the impression of inaction. On the contrary, we shall resist to our utmost strength— till we exhaust the limit of our moral, mental and intellectual capacities, but without the use of physical force or violence.

Gourgey: What does that mean in practice?

Khan: It means that we would try to reason with the authorities to see the justice of our cause. But if they are not so persuaded, we shall not lift a little finger to resist them if they bodily arrest us and push us behind bars.

Gourgey: If it came to that, then your cause is lost!

Khan: Not necessarily. Others will take up our cause. Public opinion will be aroused. Agitation through the press, platform and Parliament and in the Legislative Assembly will be vigorously conducted by our supporters. Mass countrywide meetings will be organised. So loud will be the voice of the people that the authorities will sooner or later be forced to release us, and appreciate the justice of our cause. This is what happened in Gandhi's mass, non-violent campaigns of 1922, 1931 and 1942. Alongside these campaigns, the Congress followed what Gandhiji called the 'Constructive Programme' and it is vitally important to remember this aspect of our freedom movement. But as I was explaining: these campaigns were preceded and followed by periods of non-cooperation, that is, by the non-payment of taxes, resignation from government posts, the renunciation of titles and honours, boycott of foreign goods and purchase of *swadeshi* or domestic goods and *khadi* or homespun cloth. This is what Gandhiji also called 'civil disobedience' aimed at undermining the authority of, and causing disrespect to, the foreign government and its system of law and order. When you deliberately break the law you strike at the very roots of the governmental system.

Gourgey: Say if in the Courts of Justice you are found guilty and sentenced to imprisonment?

Khan: At the trial we personally shall offer no defence. We are confident that truth will prevail. Our faith in our cause will ultimately be justified. We shall be prepared to accept the maximum punishment imposed by the law.

Gourgey: Will you then accept years of imprisonment?

Khan: Gladly. If we are in the wrong by breaking the law we deserve imprisonment. Gandhi had prison sentences for eight years. Nehru for fourteen years! Perhaps they are the better for it! Justice is Truth in Action. Whoever violates Truth must be prepared to suffer for it. That is not martyrdom, that is commonsense. Martyrs are those who are made to suffer by the authorities who know that they themselves are in the wrong in the passing of the sentence and in the manner of its execution.

Gourgey: Getting back to the mutiny, how do you think it will end?

Khan: I don't know how it will end. I know only how I want it to end. That is, for the authorities to deal with our demands fully and fairly.

Gourgey: You may be held responsible for starting the mutiny.

Khan: I agree. We are prepared for gaol.

Gourgey: I don't know if you are being sensible, but you have plenty of courage.

Khan: We need it. Non-violent methods in defence require a higher degree of moral courage than the use of violence. When attacked violently one instinctively wants to defend oneself violently. The ordinary law allows the use of force necessary for self-defence. But the higher moral law of non-violence enjoins self-restraint and self-control. This is more difficult.

Gourgey: Then you might allow yourself to be killed?

Khan: Non-violence requires self-sacrifice. True *satyagrahis* must be prepared to pay the supreme price. But before doing so, we shall strain to our utmost to convert our adversary to appreciate our point of view. Such conversion is our constant purpose.

25

Gourgey: Your purpose is defeated if you are killed!

Khan: We might have been killed anyway! In which case, there is no chance of the enemy being converted. But if he has killed non-violent resisters, there is hope of his seeing the error of his ways, leading to repentance and ultimate conversion. Then our sacrifice would have benefited not ourselves but our community and our children.

Gourgey: But if you would have used force, you would have had an equally good chance of defeating your enemy . . .

Khan: That depends on circumstances. Supposing you do win, it's a hollow victory. Violence breeds violence and the spirit of vengeance. In the First World War the superior military might of the Allies eventually defeated Germany. Then Germany was filled with the desire for vengeance. The result was the evil of Hitler and the Second World War, just twenty years later!

Gourgey: Hitler was destroyed! And there was an ideal, or the moral force of Freedom to back up the military force.

Khan: Such a philosophy of violence inevitably led to this terrible War, bringing death and destruction to millions. But with this philosophy, Hitler too believed, rightly or wrongly, he was fighting for Germany's freedom. So if two nations, sincerely believing in their ultimate ideals, feel that only the clash of arms will resolve the clash of ideals, there is no hope for humanity! As we see now in the invention of the atom bomb, modern military science has made defence for one nation seem offence to another!

But if they accept the philosophy of non-violence, there will be no limit to their patiently negotiating and seeking to reconcile their conflicting views. Humanity will at least have breathing space, if not agreement! Thus the peaceful settlement of international, and indeed, individual disputes can be achieved.

You say Britain believes she fought for Freedom. How can Indian nationalists believe this to be so when Britain gave no guarantee of India's freedom?

Gourgey: The whole aim of British colonialism is to train dependent territories for self-government.

Khan: The principle of colonialism, British or other, is bad because it denies equality and freedom to nations and to individuals. It hinders the development of their particular genius, best expressed in freedom. The sooner colonialism ends the better! Genuine independence, which India wants, is best! History has shown that British colonialists only part with power when forced to do so, as was the case with the United States of America.

Gourgey: This is not quite true in the case of some other countries like Canada, Australia and New Zealand.

Khan: Firstly, these were European peoples, mainly of Anglo-Saxon origin. Secondly, the use of force or threat of its use, has been the final deciding factor! Yet if Britain transfers sovereign power to India in peaceful agreement with Indian nationalists, we believe a new hope and a new force will be created for all subject nations.

Gourgey: To whom will Britain transfer power? Hindus or Muslims?

Khan: This will be arranged in negotiations, and conferences between the various leaders concerned. If India is partitioned – as in 1940 Jinnah and the Muslim League said they want a separate Muslim State of Pakistan – that is India's own internal affair. If there is to be civil war between Hindus and Muslims this is no excuse for withholding independence. It is no worse than the precedent of British history, where before the United Kingdom became united there was much fighting between the English themselves and later the Scots, the Welsh and the Irish, all of whom the English crushed. And then Ireland was partitioned and the Irish Free State created in 1922. I am an Indian Muslim and I trust our leaders.

Gourgey: You said the sooner colonialism ends the better! But timing for self-government is an important factor. How can Britain relinquish power if the dependent peoples are not prepared for it?

Khan: What is the criterion for such preparedness? Is it education? If so, to what extent? What about the degree of industrial and agricultural development? The provision of essential services, public administration, defence, communications'etc.? How do you decide when the people are in a position to exercise independent judgement and make sound decisions? These were certainly not done in the appeasement of Hitler and Mussolini in the thirties! Two world wars in thirty years causing death at the hand of man to over fifty million men, women and children – the greatest and cruellest destruction in history – had their cause and origin in Europe. There is no real answer to these questions. If the same criteria were adopted for European nations, many should still be denied sovereign power!

Gourgey: The mutiny has set loose forces of communist subversion among the civilian populace.

27

Khan: We are not responsible for that! Communism breeds where the needs of the masses are unfulfilled. Where there exists poverty, hunger and ignorance. Communists will seek to exploit any such situation. The authorities can best meet the communist challenge by providing for the needs of the masses. In our Central Strike Committee we reject communists and their methods. Communism means subservience to Moscow. They bring a sham independence. It is also shameful! We won't exchange one set of imperialist masters for another! But you must be clever to outwit communists. They play a subtle game. And it is in the minds and hearts of men. To win, you must meet and defeat them on their own ground. Brute force is certainly not enough. This is where non-violence is best! It calls for soul-force and intellectual ability. With this weapon we can defeat colonialists and communists!

Gourgey: Gandhi's teaching about truth and non-violence requires you to have the courage of your convictions.

Khan: Not only that! You need supreme faith and supreme moral courage. Gandhiji himself would sooner die than hurt a fly! The West does not appreciate his philosophy, which is more simple than subtle. The masses of India understand Gandhi. That is why they follow him.

Gourgey: But they have no arms . . .

Khan: They can acquire these arms, somehow, if they wish. About thirty years ago, no one believed the poor masses of Russia could ever overthrow the all-powerful Tsar. But the communists did it, by violence, which Lenin taught them was the only way.

Gourgey: So you believe that Gandhi's faith in non-violence will win through.

Khan: Absolutely. It is the only way. All depends on faith.

Gourgey: As a Jew, I believe Faith and Reason are not contradictory. Indeed there is a reason underlying faith. This you can trace to the First Cause of Creation. Despite the theory of evolution, a Supreme Being *created* the first atom, the first impulse of life, of being . . . Science discovers the laws which Religion knows to exist. Ultimately, through religion or science one must come to the Eternal Source of all the universe. Faith in God, faith in oneself, faith in one's cause, will conquer·all. If you have such faith, I believe you will win.

Khan: I agree. It is the true path and the path of truth.

Discussion over, we went home.

6

Day Four

On Thursday morning I reported for duty at RIN headquarters in Mint Road and was told to go to the CCO to replace members of the skeleton staff who had remained there overnight.

I recognised a number of fellow-officers from Castle Barracks. Their presence was desirable in view of their personal knowledge of the mutinying ratings in Castle Barracks, several of whom served on their staffs. In the event of an emergency like the previous one, they were well placed to exercise a restraining influence.

While in the CCO, we received information that the mutineers were becoming increasingly restless. We heard, too, that further troops had been rushed up to reinforce those whom we had noticed earlier at the outer gates of Castle Barracks. Viewing the scene from a side-window in the CCO, I saw a number of ratings pacing the ramparts, armed with Sten guns. Suddenly the two huge doors of the Barracks swung wide open. Ratings charged through them, this time armed with rifles and bayonets.

The situation became precarious. From my vantage-point in the CCO, I could see troops taking up their former positions guarding the outer gates.

Learning from their previous experience, the ratings quickly took shelter in the hutments on both sides of the road and started sniping at the troops. Our position in the CCO now became more risky as the mutinying snipers blocked the road linking us with the troops. I leaned out of the window as far as possible to get a better view, when I heard a shout from the ramparts. I recognised one of my men vigorously signalling to me to take cover, and as I did so, I heard the whistling sound of a stream of bullets rush past the place where my head was a second earlier.

Sensing the trapped position into which we had allowed ourselves to fall by remaining in the CCO, we grabbed rifles and bayonets. Our telephone line with HQ suddenly went dead as we were reporting the new situation. The steady crackle of rifle fire rang out as mutineers in the hutments and on the ramparts exchanged shots with the troops.

We had a conference with the Senior Officer present, when various suggestions were mooted as to how to get out of the trap. One suggestion was for a few of us to make a break for it while the others gave covering fire. This was dismissed as incurring unnecessary risks.

Another was to open fire on mutineers in the Barracks to show that we were armed and thus discourage possible attempts at forcing the entrance to the CCO. After considerable discussion, this plan too was shelved as offering too much provocation to the ratings who had so far left the CCO intact.

One of us suggested to the Senior Officer that the white flag should be waved, preparatory to an attempt to negotiate with the mutineers.

The Senior Officer turned on him savagely, and in a voice hoarse with rage, shouted: "Surrender? Never! The prestige of the British Empire is at stake! We'll see these mutineers hanged before we yield an inch. The only way to treat these bastards is to show them who is their master! To give in to them would be setting a dangerous example for the whole Empire. Never, never surrender to these swines!"

It was explained to the Senior Officer that eventually negotiations would have to take place between the authorities and mutineers everywhere if wholesale massacre and destruction were to be avoided. (As we shall see later, it very nearly came to this for all naval mutineers!)

But the Senior Officer refused to hear any more of this suggestion. How poor, indeed tragic, his judgement was became evident four or five hours later when precisely this suggestion was adopted. But this time it originated from RIN headquarters itself, with a white flag to signal a truce and a very senior officer included in the delegation from HQ to negotiate a local settlement with the mutineers in the Barracks. The tragedy lay in the fact that in the course of the four- or five-hour interval, one officer was killed – shot while on the roof of a building near HQ – and some ratings injured in the exchange of shots. Considerations of imperial prestige proved unnecessarily expensive.

One way or another, the mutineers were mainly contained in the Barracks, though some had already gained possession of several small ships covered by guns.

Sporadic firing continued till the afternoon. People had to be evacuated from the vicinity of Castle Barracks because of the danger of stray bullets. Firing was directed at the dockyard from ships in the harbour brought under the control of the mutineers. Some trained Oerlikon guns on the Burma Shell heavy oil depot on the harbour front but little damage was caused.

Vice-Admiral Sir John Godfrey, FOCRIN arrived during the day from Delhi to take personal command of the situation in Bombay. Prior to his arrival, the Flag Officer, Bombay had issued orders that unless all ratings returned to their establishments by the afternoon they would be arrested.

Indian troops supported by the Bombay City Police rounded up over forty seamen who had refused to return to establishments or ships in accordance with naval orders.

Many strikers obeyed the orders broadcast from lorries roving the streets, including those at *Talwar*. A meeting of the Central Strike Committee consisting of representatives of thirty-two ships and shore establishments was held at the Signal Training School in the morning. The meeting appointed a sub-committee of five to conduct negotiations with the naval authorities. Some ships removed Congress and Muslim League flags which they had flown at the outbreak of the mutiny.

The FOCRIN issued a statement later that night:

> It is not possible to estimate the number of ratings who are still at large. The military were called out to furnish pickets at the gates of various shore establishments but after a period of comparative quiet during the late afternoon yesterday, ratings in Castle Barracks tried to rush the pickets. The situation appears to be quieter though it remains extremely tense.

Meanwhile the situation everywhere, particularly in its civilian aspect, was worsening dangerously.

More chaos spread into Bombay city as crowds smashed shop windows and attacked, burned and over-turned tramcars and buses. Several people were injured and the civil police were compelled to open fire.

In the bazaar and mill areas, four branches of the Imperial Bank were burned down. So was the military air booking centre opposite the Bombay Government Secretariat in the Fort area.

British armoured cars and troops arrived from Poona and began to reinforce the police in the city, although they were too few to do much more than patrol in lorries with their arms at the ready. The civil police had already been compelled to open fire, injuring three people.

Casualties admitted to military hospitals were: one Royal Navy officer and two ratings, injured, two RIN officers (one of whom died), seven British Army other ranks and one RAF other rank.

Lieut-General R.M.M. Lockhart, General Officer Commanding, Southern Command, India flew into Bombay. GHQ, New Delhi made the following announcement:

> In accordance with the orders of General Sir Claude Auckinleck, who is of course Commander-in-Chief in India of the Royal Indian Navy, the Army in India, the Royal Air Force and the Royal Indian Air Force, General Lockhart has assumed command of all forces of these Services in the area. He has been charged with restoring order in the Royal Indian Navy as rapidly as possible.

It was officially announced later by GHQ, Delhi, that strong military, naval and air reinforcements were sent to Karachi, Poona and Bombay in view of the naval mutiny.

The Governor of Bombay, Sir John Colville, maintained close touch with the Service chiefs. At the highest level the Viceroy, Lord Wavell, and his Executive Council were in constant contact with the Commander-in-Chief, General Sir Claude Auckinleck.

At RIN barracks in New Delhi, thirty-eight ratings who had returned to duty were arrested by the military authorities and investigations were initiated to take a decision on disciplinary action.

In HMIS *Hooghly* at Calcutta, the strike by naval ratings continued and civilian transport drivers had joined in. New demands were presented. They included revision of an order for the dismissal of a telegraphist in *Talwar* called Dutt (whose home was in Calcutta), the withdrawal of military guards from naval establishments in Bombay and Karachi, and the release of all those who had been arrested anywhere in connection with the disturbances.

In Bombay harbour many RIN vessels were under the control of the ratings. They had the guns on board trained on important landmarks along Bombay's skyline—especially on the Royal Yacht Club and the Taj Mahal Hotel. These were also the centres of "European pomp and show": that they were likely targets was not without significance!

It was only by the late evening that those of us who had been trapped in the CCO were able to leave. In fact, this was the first point in the local settlement referred to above. But the settlement involved the central issue of surrender by the mutineers to the authorities. Since Castle Barracks was the main point of resistance in shore establishments, the settlement provided a pattern for the other establishments. The terms of the settlement included the unconditional surrender of all mutineers as required by the naval authorities. For their part, the latter expressed readiness to give full and early consideration to the ratings' grievances, the main one concerning speedy demobilisation and resettlement plans in civilian life. Although the surrender was to be unconditional, it was felt that an expression of readiness to consider grievances would be taken as a sign of the authorities' *bona fides*, which would be conducive to a calmer atmosphere. Arising out of the mutiny, however, and at the insistence of Congress leaders, the authorities had to make a 'gentlemen's agreement' that there would be no victimisation of the strike leaders. Nevertheless, the fact that the Congress party was now showing an increasing reluctance to support the mutiny, by not calling for a mass *satyagraha* and civil disobedience campaign, discouraged the ratings' leaders from continuing with the mutiny.

Congress party leaders, including Sardar Vallabhai Patel, publicly deplored the situation in the city and appealed to every responsible person to see that peace was restored between the parties and that Bombay city was not plunged into trouble. He further stated that the Congress party was doing everything to help naval ratings out of their difficulties.

For the following day, Friday, a general stoppage of work or *hartal* had been scheduled by the Congress as it was the anniversary of the death of Kasturba Gandhi, the beloved wife of the Mahatma, who had died in gaol after revolutionary incidents had broken out all over the country in 1942 when the Congress was declared to be an illegal organisation on the passing of the 'Quit India' resolution.

However, as a result of their bitter experiences of past disturbances, the Congress leaders called off the proposed stoppage of work which would have aggravated the situation even more.

All the officers of Castle Barracks were required to report for duty at RIN headquarters and the CCO, late on the evening of Day Four, for various missions.

One of these was to split up into units of two officers accompanied by two military policemen touring the city in a jeep and rounding up roving gangs of mutinying sailors.

Another far more prosaic job was to sort out from among the records kept at HQ the cases of those ratings with long-standing requests for leave or release or grants of pay and prepare suitable recommendations for settling such requests.

Yet another was to try and intercept signals between mutineers in shore establishments to gauge their reaction to the state of siege imposed upon them by the military authorities. For in several shore establishments, the Army Commander of the locality was ordered to cordon off the establishment by troops, to prevent ratings from joining together in bigger groups and entering the city.

The task assigned to me was, with others, to tap telephone wires between shore establishments which were all connected with HQ on separate lines. In this way, I listened in to a conversation between ratings in a shore establishment which was a torpedo training base and another establishment which gave training in 'Asdics' (anti-submarine detection devices).

A rating in the torpedo training base who, it transpired, was a member of its Strike Committee, was recounting the day's incidents to another rating in the 'Asdics' centre.

"We have prevented three of our officers from leaving the establishment," he disclosed. "While they are comfortable in the mess, we have an armed guard at the door. They would be useful as hostages if the authorities instruct the troops to try and take over the establishment," he added.

"Keep them there!" the other replied. "We were told this afternoon by *Talwar* that plans are made for prolonging the mutiny, if the Congress will not satisfy our strike leaders about representing our grievances to the authorities."

"Personally, I would prefer to negotiate through Aruna Asaf Ali who is in the Congress extreme left wing," the first rating said. "She has already taken a prominent part in guiding our strike leaders as to how to frame their demands and arouse the support of others, both ratings and civilians."

"Whatever our leaders do," exclaimed the other bitterly, "I hope they make sure that those white bastards will no longer dominate us—either in the Navy or in the country itself! In the present state of the siege, we can easily hold out for at least a week. Our Strike Committee has successfully managed to have ratings continue with their previous jobs, electing their leader to supervise the work and report about his responsibility to the Strike Committee. It meets in the CO's office once in the morning and once in the late afternoon."

At this stage, I asked a fellow-officer to take over my 'listening post' and I hurried along to a senior officer to report the conversation. It indicated the kind of organisation that had been set up by the ratings themselves after they had assumed control of their establishments.

The ratings, far from being demoralised by the siege and the arrival of troop reinforcements, were deriving confidence from their success at running the establishment. Thus, given an adequacy of food and water supplies – they had both victualling depots and storage tanks – they could endure a siege for quite some time. The authorities must have considered it necessary to have recourse to drastic action. And this became evident as the events of the following day showed.

7

Day Five

As a result of the settlement arrived at the previous evening in Castle Barracks, for the first time in three days we were enabled to go to our offices and survey the damage done.

There was a desolate air about everything. The Barracks had lost its usual smart appearance. Refuse littered the huge quarter-deck. Offices were unswept and papers were strewn all over desks and chairs. In several, the doors were battered in, barely hanging on by their hinges. The ratings' canteen had been ransacked and many empty tins were lying about.

The clothing stores, or 'slops', was comparatively intact owing to a sense of responsibility exercised by some of the senior ratings on the office staff who had bravely prevented pilfering by their more hot-headed comrades.

The Commanding Officer, Captain H.R. Inigo-Jones, who had the rank of Captain and was a 'regular' in the Royal Indian Navy, grimly surveyed the depressing scene. Who knows what thoughts he must have had about this important establishment which he had efficiently commanded for some years, now reduced almost to a shambles? But the needs of the moment demanded his immediate attention. Turning to his First Lieutenant, Lieut-Commander Scott, in a brisk voice he ordered: "Please have the Strike Committee report to my office in an hour. I want to investigate a number of things."

Turning on his heel, he strode off to his office.

A little while later, a number of officers on his staff were summoned to give preliminary reports on the condition of the ratings and offices in their charge. The general tenor of these reports was the demoralisation that had set in amongst the ratings and the need to restore speedily their sense of discipline and confidence in the Service. Easier said than done! For the clear understanding and trust that had previously prevailed was now bedevilled by the spirit of national revolution that was in the air, and the radical political changes impending as a result of the forthcoming Cabinet Mission visit to India. Moreover, the mutiny had dealt a severe blow to Britain's military prestige in India, now undergoing a rapid decline, which had begun after the INA trials.

The difficulty of restoring discipline became more evident to the CO after the meeting with the Strike Committee. It confirmed earlier impressions of the resentment felt by ratings at the way in which *they* imagined their grievances were being handled. As the Strike Committee left his office, I heard the CO mutter disconsolately: "I wish someone would bring Punnu Khan here to talk to these fellows." I undertook to do so in view of the acquaintance I had previously struck up with him.

I climbed into a jeep and instructed the driver to proceed to *Talwar*. *En route*, I could not help but notice the destruction at the dockyard where we paused to refuel and the rather mechanical air of the ratings and civilian workers as they went about their ordinary duties. The events of the past few days had seemed like a nightmare from which we were gradually emerging.

At *Talwar* itself the atmosphere seemed still more unreal. For the mutineers knew now that there was no longer any chance of prolonging the mutiny to secure quick redressal for their grievances. Furthermore, the troop reinforcements that had been rushed to Bombay from all over India, and from bases abroad, were overwhelmingly superior to the forces at the disposal of the mutineers.

I asked the Executive Officer to allow Punnu Khan to be taken under escort to Castle Barracks and explained the CO's purpose. Looking rather suspicious, the strike leader sat at the rear of the jeep.

"Why are you taking me to Castle, sir?" he asked, with what seemed a certain sharpness in his voice. "It's nothing to worry about," I answered him. "The CO will explain to you when we get there."

Appearing somewhat relieved, he relaxed a little in his seat.

As we sped along I asked for his views on the outcome of the mutiny.

"Well, sir," he declared emphatically, "we feel it is a good thing that it happened. At least the authorities know now that they have to deal properly with our problems."

"What about the civilian disturbances?" I enquired further.

"As you know," he commented, "we had little or nothing to do with them. Nationalism and continuing foreign rule have inflamed the masses."

"What do you expect to happen to you and the other mutineers in the immediate future?"

"We are not quite sure. We expect to be charged and found guilty of mutiny. But whether we shall have light or heavy sentences will depend on the Congress. They have promised to do their best for us. At least there should not be any victimisation of the leaders."

"What will you do if there is victimisation?"

"We shall wait to see if that happens," he retorted grimly, and his finely-drawn features hardened.

We were approaching Castle Barracks now, and the sentry at the outer gates saluted me, and gave a quick nod of recognition to Khan as he smilingly waved to him.

The ratings in Castle Barracks had somehow got wind of his arrival and thronged the entrance as he drove through, cheering wildly and waving their caps. It was more like a triumphal procession for him than being brought under escort at the command of the CO! But any member of the Central Strike Committee and the delegation which negotiated 'as equals' with the top ranking naval officers received a hero's welcome.

Khan was taken to the CO's office where he was told of the demoralised attitude of the men. He himself realised the need to instil confidence in them, if only to steel them for difficult days ahead when investigations and trials were likely to be held. But little did he know how soon they would be made to realise that the tide had now turned against them.

Shortly after he had ended his talk to the erstwhile mutineers a signal was received from HQ that Admiral Godfrey himself (FOCRIN) was going to broadcast a most important message that afternoon from All India Radio, Bombay to all ratings, and ships and establishments everywhere were required to listen in. In Castle Barracks the loudhailer system was checked and the ratings assembled on the quarter-deck.

Punctually at 2.00 p.m., Admiral Godfrey's voice came over the air, loud and clear. Expressing his deep personal sorrow at the recent events in the Royal Indian Navy, the Admiral declared: "I must tell you that the Government has vast forces at its disposal with which to crush the mutiny. It will accept nothing but unconditional surrender on your part. If this is not forthcoming immediately, the Government will proceed to employ all its forces against those who still mutiny."

At the famous words 'unconditional surrender', the ratings listened with rapt attention.

"I warn you against further resistance," the Admiral went on , "and advise you to lay down your arms now. The Government is determined to bring this situation to an end," he paused significantly here and then continued "even if it means *the destruction of the Navy of which we have all been so proud.*"

At this last statement a gasp of incredulity went up from the entire assembly, including the officers. Many of the old veterans, both amongst officers and ratings, could scarcely conceal the tears in their eyes. For it was as if a part of them was being wrenched away, blacked out. This Service, to which they had devoted the greater part of their lives, and with which their thoughts and feelings had been so intimately bound, stood now in danger of imminent destruction. Perhaps it was a measure of the epochal times through which they lived that such a thing was not only contemplated but well within the bounds of possibility.

It was all over! After the broadcast the mutineers in all ships and establishments realised that it was futile to carry on. A profound sense of disillusionment was unavoidable. For the mutiny had doubtless conjured up visions of speedy demobilisation, return to 'civvy street' and their homes and families and a satisfactory settlement of their pay and other problems.

These visions faded at the prospect of abject and total surrender to overwhelmingly superior military forces. The virtual disavowal of the mutiny by Congress leaders was also a source of disappointment, though it was realised that the mutiny was neither organised by, nor figured in the plans of the Congress to gain independence.

Several ships now signalled the authorities their intention to surrender and await further instructions. Yet on some others there were the more hot-headed members of the crew who were all for fighting on. They believed that the Government would be extremely reluctant to carry out its threat, and that continued resistance would secure advantageous terms before drastic action such as bombing their ships would be taken. Furthermore, they believed that indignant public opinion would force the hand of Congress leaders to strive harder for to attain their goals. But these ideas were harshly dispelled when nineteen RAF planes flew over Bombay city as the Admiral issued another proclamation:

> I told you that ample forces are available to restore order. The General Officer Commanding, Southern Command, General Lockhart, has been ordered by His Excellency the C-in-C, General Sir Claude Auckinleck, to assume supreme control in Bombay. To show you that ample forces are available, he has ordered a formation of RAF aircraft to fly over the harbour. These aircraft will not fly over ships nor take any offensive action provided there is no action taken against them. Should you now have decided, in accordance with my warning, to surrender unconditionally, you are to hoist a large black or blue flag and muster all hands on deck on the side facing Bombay city and await further orders.

Moreover, following on the Admiral's call for 'unconditional surrender' the Central Strike Committee at *Talwar* issued their own appeal. They stated that they had been in direct and constant contact with Sardar Vallabhai Patel who had been mainly responsible for making the Congress easily the largest, most efficient and effective political party in India and perhaps in Asia. Mr Patel had repeated on the night before that the mutineers must give in unconditionally and trust to Congress efforts to deal with their grievances and prevent victimisation. This advice the Committee finally accepted.

A hint of Mr Patel's advice had been dropped by those members of the Strike Committee who were drawn from various ships and establishments, though the official appeal of the Strike Committee was awaited.

It was not to be unexpected that early on Friday morning, the mutineers in possession of the *Hindustan* at Karachi were informed by a senior naval officer that military action to capture the ship would be started unless they surrendered forthwith.

The mutineers were allowed until 9.00 a.m. for any ratings who wished to do so to leave the ship. No advantage was taken of that period and at about 10.00 a.m. a senior military officer called upon the mutineers to lay down their arms and abandon ship, as this was their last chance before action to seize the ship was taken.

The mutineers were warned that any men remaining on deck who did not surrender would be fired on. The only response was that some of the mutineers manned the ship's guns on deck. At 10.35 a.m. after the period of grace had elapsed, a strictly controlled rifle fire on individuals still on the ship's deck was opened by the troops. The ship returned the fire with heavy machine guns but the military still restricted their fire to sniping by individual riflemen. At this stage another ship standing nearby, HMIS *Travancore*, put out to sea.

The company of *Hindustan* then began firing with the whole of the ship's armament including 4" guns and it became necessary to open fire in return with field guns and mortars. Hits on the deck of the ship were observed when suddenly a white flag was displayed. The troops ashore stopped firing. Two launches filled with soldiers immediately put out to sea to take control of the ship. As they approached, a rating who had manned a machine gun swivelled it around and a burst of firing broke out. Quickly a sniper on one of the launches took aim and shot the rating on board, injuring him seriously in the shoulder.

As the troops boarded the ship, they received sullen glares from the mutineers. The officer in charge rapidly took control of the situation. He ordered the ratings to drop their weapons, turn around and raise their hands above their heads, while at the point of the bayonet the soldiers shepherded them on to the quarter deck.

Reported casualties were four RIN ratings killed and twenty-six injured. One British other rank amongst the troops was wounded. The ship's company were disembarked and a military detachment occupied the vessel.

In Bombay, as elsewhere, news of the call to surrender rapidly spread. As the curfew fell at 9.00 p.m. an eerie silence descended over the greater part of Bombay. With troops, armed police, pickets and armoured cars stationed at strategic points, the wider streets were empty. In the narrower by-lanes, small gangs flashed in and out in attempts to loot shops. They disappeared on the arrival of the police, and then re-emerged to try again.

These attempts were partly successful and amongst the shops looted were twenty-eight grain shops. The war-time rationing question still remained unsolved and resulting food shortages aggravated mob anger. The blame for the large-scale civil disturbances was laid at the door of the communists and the Congress socialists by official Congress leaders who stated there was a deliberate intention to discredit the party and Mahatma Gandhi.

Reports collated about the civil upheaval indicated the widespread violence which accompanied the disturbances, and also the enormous numbers involved. At one point in the mill area, during the day, police patrols were trying to cope with a mass of wildly excited rioters, estimated by some observers at thirty thousand. One policeman was killed and two police officers injured before a military party arrived and dispersed the mob with fire. In this area alone, some hundred and fifty people were wounded of whom thirty later died. In the notorious Bhendy Bazaar area a violent attack all but overwhelmed a police party including three officers, from two of whom revolvers were forcibly taken. Total police casualties then numbered thirty officers and ninety constables injured. Three of the latter died shortly afterwards. Estimated figures of civilian casualties were five hundred injured and sixty dead.

The last day of actual fighting by naval mutineers ended with grim forebodings of the future. The mutiny had set in motion a series of events which could have the gravest consequences. Many of its leaders had serious apprehensions as to their individual fate, since the Congress had not made common cause with them as much as they had done with the prisoners, especially Captain Shah Nawaz, in the INA trials of the previous year. Despite the assurances of Congress leaders, victimisation was a fear uppermost in the minds of prominent mutineers. They had no doubt that they would undergo a period of detention, but they were more concerned about the nature and timing of the forthcoming trials.

The mutiny had nevertheless made a deep impression on the minds of political leaders at all levels, and this was the case not least in the Central Legislative Assembly at New Delhi, and to some extent in the House of Commons.

8

In Parliament and Assembly

The first reference to the mutiny in the House of Commons was made on February 22, when Mr Henderson Stewart (Fife E., L. Nat.) asked leave to move the adjournment of the House "on a definite matter of urgent public importance, namely the grave extension of the mutiny among sections of the Royal Indian Navy, which now were reported to have seized twenty-four ships."

In reply, the Prime Minister, Mr Attlee, stated:

> I have had no notice that the Hon. Member was going to raise this question and I have not at present any information from the Government of India. The only information I have comes from naval sources which state that certain vessels of the Royal Navy are proceeding towards Bombay.[1] I suggest that if the House would wait until I get some information, I will give it to them then and that it would be for the House then to consider whether they would like to raise the matter.

Mr Henderson Stewart apologised for the short notice and said he did not wish to embarrass the Government or to make the position more serious. Perhaps the Prime Minister would undertake, if he received news later in the day, to interrupt the proceedings in order to give it, or to make a statement at the beginning of the proceedings the next day.

---

1. These were the cruiser *Glasgow* and two destroyers.

Mr Attlee said that he had telegraphed urgently to India but had not received any reply yet:

> I do not know whether I shall get one today. I hope that by the opening of the House tomorrow I might be able to make a full statement. I have explained that I have not full information on this matter. I understand there has been some firing. I am not certain what the craft are, but the RIN are not under the command of the Admiralty. They come under the Commander-in-Chief in India and under the admiral acting under him. They are not primarily concerned with the First Lord of the Admiralty.

Mr Henderson Stewart withdrew his motion.

On February 23, Mr Attlee gave to the House a summary of the incidents which had already occurred. After outlining the day-to-day developments in the mutiny when on Thursday "the mutineers were reported to be mainly contained in the barracks, but some are in possession of several small ships which are covered by guns", he went on:

> The Governor reported last night that the city remained calm so far with little trouble except some natural alarm in areas close to the docks.
>
> The Congress party officially disclaimed participation in the mutiny, but left-wing elements and Communists were trying to work up sympathy and it is anticipated that there will be more trouble before the situation is stabilised . . . General Lockhart, the Commander of the Southern Army, is now GOC-in-C of all the forces in Bombay. The Viceroy and his Council are in the closest touch with the Commander-in-Chief.
>
> The mutineers have been told that only unconditional surrender will be accepted. Ample forces are available in Bombay and Karachi, where there has been some fighting between Royal Indian naval ratings in one of His Majesty's Indian ships at the quay and the forces on shore. Ships of the Royal Navy, including a cruiser, are proceeding to the scene and will very shortly arrive.
>
> I know the House will feel deep regret that this should have occurred in the Royal Indian Navy which did such magnificent service in the War. We all hope that wiser counsels will prevail. Meanwhile, order must be restored.

Mr R.A. Butler said the Opposition shared the views the Prime Minister had expressed about the magnificent service of the Royal Indian Navy during the War and he hoped that Mr Attlee also realised that he had their support in backing the authorities on the spot to restore order and in demanding the unconditional surrender of the mutineers.

Mr Callaghan asked, as one who had seen something of service in the Royal Indian Navy, that an early investigation should take place.

In an editorial headlined "Bombay to Cairo", *The Times* said, *inter alia*:

> Mr Attlee's statement in Parliament made it clear that a large proportion of the ratings of the Royal Indian Navy had been in open mutiny since Monday. Whatever were their grievances on the subjects of pay, rations and demobilisation, the refusal of duty preceded any formulation of demands for their redress. The Prime Minister told the House that the Congress party had officially disclaimed the mutiny and indeed it was hardly conceivable that a movement which hopes to be carrying the full burden of Government should have wished to condone in any way an outburst of gross indiscipline which, if tolerated, would undermine the very foundations of the State. It is therefore no surprise to hear that on the advice of a leader of the Congress party the mutineers have decided to surrender unconditionally . . .

The Times also reported that "official Congress leaders bitterly charge the Communists and Congress Socialists with inspiring the whole distressing tragedy with the deliberate intention of discrediting the party and Mr Gandhi".

The tense political situation which continued to exist, and of which the mutiny was a symptom, doubtless caused the Prime Minister to make a decisive statement on India's future.

Shortly after his statement on the mutiny, Mr Attlee announced in the Commons a decision by the Government, with the King's approval, to send to India towards the end of March a special mission of Cabinet Ministers, consisting of Lord Pethwick-Lawrence,[1] Sir Stafford Cripps,[2] and Mr A.V. Alexander.[3] They were to act in association with the Viceroy in discussions with leaders of Indian opinion on problems arising out of the early realisation by India of self-government. The steps to be taken included: 1) preparatory discussions with the elected representatives of British India, and with the Indian States,

---

1. The Secretary of State for India.
2. The President of the Board of Trade, who made the famous 'Cripps Proposals' to Indian leaders in 1942 at the direction of the then Prime Minister, Mr Winston Churchill.
3. The First Lord of the Admiralty.

in order to secure the widest measure of agreement as to the method of framing a constitution; 2) setting up of a constitution-making body; and 3) bringing into being of an Executive Council having the support of the main Indian parties.

A similar statement was made in the House of Lords by Lord Pethwick-Lawrence.

In the Commons, Mr Anthony Eden elicited from the Prime Minister the information that the three ministers would have powers to negotiate with Indian leaders within the terms laid down by the Cabinet decision. Clearly, Mr Attlee said, anything arising out of the discussions would be subject to legislation and would come before the House.

Lord Pethwick-Lawrence in the House of Lords, answering questions by Lord Simon and Lord Samuel, said that the Cabinet delegation would assist in setting up the constitution-making body in India and that the Viceroy's hands would be strengthened by their presence. It was for the Indian people to decide on the basis of their constitutional structure.

Lord Simon referred to "this most important statement and highly novel procedure" and said that they all joined in the hope that the plan might bear fruit, and that it might be regarded in India as a proof of the genuine desire of Britain to help towards the solution of India's intractable constitutional problems.

Commenting on the situation, *The Times* stated that the announcement of the visit to India of the three Cabinet Ministers was quietly received in Parliament:

> where there is no disposition to underestimate the difficult and delicate nature of the mission. It recognises that India is at a critical stage, and that the present discontent may easily be exacerbated by famine . . . It is becoming clear that even if the prior consent of all parties to participate, which is by far the best assurance of the constitution-making process, cannot be realised, that defect cannot be allowed indefinitely to obstruct the march of India towards self-government . . .

In its editorial, the *Manchester Guardian* stated: ". . . a stroke of courage and imagination, this step will bring home to the British people the challenge that India presents to their political capacity and good faith."

Reaction in India to the Prime Minister's statement was no less swift and no less cordial.

Maulana Abul Kalam Azad, President of the Congress party, stated that the British Government's decision to send a delegation of Cabinet Ministers to India would be appreciated by the country. He added that he was "specially pleased to learn that Sir Stafford Cripps is to be a member of the delegation".

Dealing with the mutiny and its repercussions in civilian life, Maulana Azad said:

> In the present atmosphere of the country which is surcharged with emotion and political irritation, it is essential that nothing should be done which may aggravate the situation. I earnestly appeal to the authorities concerned to try and see things from the Indian national point of view. India is not in a mood to tolerate any action that may have even the semblance of suppression of the national spirit in any quarter.

Maulana Azad warned that if nothing concrete emerged from the Cabinet Mission, plans would have to be considered for a "final overthrow".

Sardar Vallabhai Patel, who ranked after Nehru in the Congress hierarchy, in a statement quoted earlier, referred to the mutiny and the forthcoming Cabinet Ministers' visit:

> . . . It was not without the greatest difficulty that I persuaded the ratings to surrender unconditionally,[1] giving them at the same time the assurance that whatever was just in their cause would be championed by the Congress, that so far as was humanly possible, full justice would be done and that there would be no victimisation. I am only hoping that authority will not hark back to old worn-out methods and senselessly insist on former prestige . . .
>
> We have been looking forward to the coming of the official deputation and only hope that it is coming with the determined purpose of withdrawing British rule from all India and laying the foundations of a lasting friendship between Great Britain and India while there is yet a moment left.

He concluded with the significant warning: "Let not history record that it was too late."

Speaking for 'Princely' India i.e., non-British India divided into approximately five hundred Indian States in separate treaty relationships with the Crown, the Nawab of Bhopal, who was Chancellor

---

1. Mr Jinnah, the Muslim League President, also tendered the same advice to a deputation of ratings who sought his guidance.

of the Chamber of Princes, made a plea for compromise and mutual sacrifice for the achievement of Indian freedom. He went on:

> If we are in earnest in our demand for a free and independent India, let us ourselves lay the foundation for that freedom and independence. I stand for a free and independent India. No Indian worthy of the name would stand for anything less.

On behalf of the All India Muslim League, Mr Mohamad Ali Jinnah, its revered President, said that although the League still objected to the setting up of a single constitution-making body for India or the setting up of an Interim Government, "we shall be glad to have free and frank talks with the Ministers".

Later, when opening the League's Bengal election campaign in Calcutta, he declared: ". . . we Muslims would try to make the British Cabinet understand that there is no other way out than acceptance of Pakistan."

In addition to the far-reaching implications of the forthcoming Cabinet Mission to India, there were widespread repercussions of the mutiny in view of the highly excitable state of the country. Leaders of the Indian National Congress and later those of the All India Muslim League under Mr Mohamad Ali Jinnah were continuously inciting their followers to the mood for revolt. This mood was quickened by the thought of a possible failure of the forthcoming constitutional discussions, rendered not unlikely by the intransigent attitude overtly taken up by the parties concerned. It seemed only a miracle could avert a deadlock and consequent disaster. The authority of the British Government in India was weakening in view of its impending retirement from the vast subcontinent it had ruled for nearly two hundred years. Yet Congress and Muslim League leaders realised that though the time was opportune to whip up the feelings of their followers, these could not be allowed to get out of control.

Shortly after the outbreak of the mutiny, the Central Legislative Assembly met in an excited atmosphere. The usual question hour was dispensed with in order to devote more time to discussion of the mutiny. While Congress leaders in the Assembly justified to a certain extent the action of the ratings, their sharp criticism was reserved for the Government benches with whom they were, as they declared, in a state of "permanent opposition".

Particular indignation was expressed over Vice-Admiral Godfrey's proclaimed policy of restoring order even if it involved the destruction of the Indian Navy. Prime Minister Attlee's announcement that warships of the Royal Navy were on their way to Bombay aroused further discontent. There were mutterings of "Shame!" from the Opposition benches and Mr Asaf Ali,[1] deputy leader of the Congress party in the Assembly, protested on their behalf against the evident intention of the British to use violence "against our Navy"! He put down an adjournment motion to call attention to the "mishandling of the situation by the immediate authorities concerned, and pass a vote of censure against the Government".

After hearing a factual statement by Mr Philip Mason,[2] the Defence Secretary, who was hopeful of a settlement very shortly, Mr Asaf Ali agreed that under the circumstances and in order that nothing might be said which would make matters worse, it would be better not to have an immediate debate. However, he asked for an assurance that the mutiny would be referred to the Defence Consultative Committee of the Assembly as soon as possible. In the meanwhile, he urged, the Government should use its best endeavours to avoid the use of force and work for a peaceful settlement as a matter of principle. On the Defence Secretary's acceptance of this suggestion, it was decided that the adjournment motion should not be taken up until the following Monday.

But while this was being arranged, Congress backbenches had shown signs of growing restiveness. Members were constantly receiving reports of civil disturbances all over the country. They were finding it increasingly difficult to restrain their own doubts as to the Government's ability to check the feelings of the civilian populace, let alone those of the mutineers. There was the added danger that mutiny and disaffection would spread throughout the Armed Forces if the naval mutiny itself was not quelled in time. In fact, it was becoming known that one of the immediate causes of its outbreak was the strike in a unit of the Royal Indian Air Force a month earlier.

Shortly afterwards, on the plea that firing on HMIS *Hindustan* indicated a significant deterioration in the situation, Opposition backbenchers succeeded in bringing up the question again, and the

---

1.   In the following year, after Indian independence in August 1947, he became India's first Ambassador to Washington.

2.   Later Secretary of the Royal Institute of International Affairs at Chatham House, London.

Government was asked to arrange for a debate on the following day. The Government spokesman protested that this would be inopportune. Negotiations with Strike Committees in various establishments had reached a critical stage. However, both Opposition parties, that is, the Congress and the Muslim League, had indicated that they were in favour of an early debate which the circumstances now warranted. Confronted with such insistence, the Government yielded.

In the course of his statement, the Defence Secretary brought the House up to date with the course of events in Bombay and Karachi and gave a list of the ratings' grievances and demands. These related, Mr Mason went on, to various matters including conditions of service and demobilisation, the behaviour of officers and disciplinary action which had been taken against two ratings before the mutiny had broken out. The ratings, who presented their demands to Admiral Godfrey, added that they wished to protest against "the Indian National Army trials and the use of Indian troops in Indonesia". The Defence Secretary promised a full inquiry into the causes of the mutiny when the men resumed duty. It was a fair guess, he concluded, that what had contributed most to their sense of grievance was the higher rate of pay enjoyed by British naval ratings who worked alongside them.

The Defence Secretary was followed by the Deputy Opposition Leader, Mr Asaf Ali. He said those in charge of the Navy should have been aware of the smouldering grievances of the ratings before things came to such a pass.

"It is never useful to be insensitive to the wishes of a group subject to a common discipline and authority," he declared. He felt that the authorities had possibly provoked the mutiny by taking disciplinary measures against two ratings of whom it was said they were caught writing political slogans on a barrack-room wall, in ignorance or contempt of the ratings' real feelings.

"When the mutiny occurred," he said, "all the authorities could do was to threaten to bring guns against 'our Navy', a threat which," he declared emphatically, "the Opposition could not tolerate with equanimity".

To try and impose a military solution to a political problem would always end in disaster. At best the military solution could but be temporary, never satisfactory, and lead to further complication. It must eventually be accompanied by a political solution to have any degree of permanence. Therefore, would not the path of wisdom be in seeking to come to grips as soon as possible with the political problems, and thus avoid the delays, defeats and frustrations caused by having to resort to military measures?

Referring to the mutineers' apparent reliance on the support of political leaders, Mr Asaf Ali said that India wanted not only a good fighting machine but also a patriotic, not a mercenary, army. It was highly desirable that the armed forces be kept out of party politics.

While this was true of Congress' view of the role of the armed forces vis-a-vis politics, it was nevertheless short of the full position taken by the Congress Government on this matter, which emerges in its conclusions on the report of the Inquiry Commission considered in the next chapter.

9

Inquiry Commission Report

Soon after the end of the mutiny, and the unconditional surrender of the ratings in all ships and establishments, a series of courts-martial were held in Castle Barracks and elsewhere. The sentences passed on those convicted of mutinying ranged from mild ones such as dismissal of ship and disrating, or loss of seniority, to those of far greater severity such as dismissal with disgrace from the Service, and imprisonment. In many cases it took time for the authorities to obtain evidence during which the suspects, numbering 396, were detained in large camps especially constructed for the purpose at Mulund. This was near Bombay and I visited it on a number of occasions to assist in the enquiries being made.

While under detention, the ratings were fairly well treated, but were made to live in tents and huts surrounded by huge barbed-wire fences, manned at regular intervals by sentries on duty round the clock, with wooden towers carrying searchlights to detect attempts at escape. The detainees remained at Mulund for varying periods, depending on the degree of preparation deemed necessary for their trial.

In the early summer of 1946 the Government of India appointed a high-powered Commission of Inquiry to "determine the causes, extent and consequences of the naval mutiny". The members of the Commission were Sir Saiyid Fazal Ali, Chief Justice of the Patna High

Court, Mr Justice Mahajan of the Lahore High Court, Mr Justice Krishnaswamy Ayyangar of Cochin, Vice-Admiral W.R. Patterson, RN, the Flag Officer Commanding, East Indies Fleet and Major-General T.W. Rees, Commander of the Fourth Indian Division. The Secretary of the Commission was Lieut-Colonel Vishweshar Nath Singh.

In the month of May the Commission sat in the Bombay High Court and recorded the evidence of a number of witnesses.

Amongst the first to give evidence was Commander F.W. King of *Talwar* who, in the course of his testimony, asserted that the revolutionary and political movement behind the mutiny led to its rapid development all over India. He referred to the 'Quit India' slogan-writing on the walls of *Talwar* as evidence of the political element in the organisation of the mutiny.

Another officer, Lieut-Commander Balwant Singh, expressed his view that:

> . . . there were innumerable cases of racial discrimination in
> the Navy, and the lot of Indian officers was miserable if they
> had to work under British officers.

An Indian officer, Lieutenant Nanda, who had approached Sardar Patel in an attempt to enlist his support for the mutiny (which was refused) stated that:

> . . . against the background of grievances, heightened political
> tension, appearance of slogans on the walls of *Talwar*, and the
> apparent inability of the authorities to trace the culprits, the latter
> thought they were perfectly safe.

A most important witness was Rear-Admiral Rattray, Flag Officer, Bombay who, it was alleged, had received a letter dated February 1 – about three weeks earlier – warning him of a possible mutiny. In the course of his testimony, he stated:

> The background of the mutiny was the grievances put forward
> by the ratings, but the overriding fact, I think, was the political
> tension prevailing in the country since the end of 1945. When
> subversive elements got to work both inside and outside the
> service . . . mutiny spread.

He thought that "from the way the mutiny had spread to all ports in India and from the similarity of slogans shouted in ships, the mutiny had been pre-arranged".

He added that in the diary of one of the leading mutineers, B.C. Dutta, was recorded a resolution of a revolutionary character passed at a meeting of the Indian ex-Servicemen's Association, and extracts from certain newspaper articles. All this had led him to believe that there were subversive elements at work.

It was also thought that there existed an "anti-Indian bias amongst British officers".

The report of the Inquiry Commission was officially published in New Delhi in January 1947. Nehru's Interim Government, which had been formed in September 1946 as a result of the British Cabinet Mission negotiations earlier in the year, published its conclusions on this report. They were to the effect that: 1) officers were obliged to consider the welfare of their men before their own comfort or safety, and grievances must not be explained away; and 2) too rapid an expansion without proper provision for training of officers was unwise. The aim of the Service in peace should be to prepare for expansion in war. The Government went on to believe that "if these lessons are remembered, this tragic chapter in the history of the Royal Indian Navy may not be entirely without good result."

While the Government wished that every officer of the Royal Indian Navy should remember these lessons, they felt that:

in the present circumstances it would serve no useful purpose to dwell too much on the past or to indulge in recrimination against those who made mistakes in the stress of war and in the abnormal conditions which followed.

The Government emphasised that the task of the Royal Indian Navy was:

to build up a national service responsible to the national will, proud of its record in the War and looking forward to a fine future. In building up such a structure the first requirement is that the Service must have confidence in itself. In this undoubtedly, one of the first factors is the nationalisation of the officers' cadre.

The report criticised Flag Officer, Bombay and his officers in the mutiny which, it stated, affected more than 74 ships, 4 flotillas and 20 shore establishments resulting in 9 ratings and one officer being killed and 41 ratings and one officer wounded. But for their "omissions" it stated, "the great catastrophe might never have happened." According to the report, the officers first and foremost did not realise the gravity of the situation at a sufficiently early stage. Secondly, they failed to take early and immediate steps to re-assert authority with firmness and at the same time they failed to take sympathetic steps to alleviate complaints. The report added that the main grievances of the men were: an incorrect and extremely rosy picture "amounting in some cases to systematic deception" held out by recruiting authorities, the lack of contact between officers and ratings, and a feeling of discrimination.

The Interim Government declared its intention to take every step to put right the grievances revealed by the report, and felt confident that the Navy would "respond and that its future would be a matter of pride for the whole country".

The Inquiry Commission was unanimous in concluding that the basic cause of the mutiny was widespread discontent, mainly over a number of Service grievances which had remained unredressed for some time and had become aggravated by the political situation.

With reference to politics, the Government of India expressed its belief that:

[a] healthy interest in the affairs of the country is to be encouraged, but the use of politics as a lever to get the grievances redressed was highly dangerous and must be discouraged in the interests of the Service . . . officers and men are being instructed that, although every man is entitled to his personal views, participation in party politics is not admissible to members of such a Service.

The Government concurred in the view of the Commission that many of the causes from which the mutiny arose were due to overrapid expansion. Naval Headquarters recommended that an adequate safety margin of regular officers and ratings should be created in peace time in the training, drafting and leave reserves, and that an efficient training force must be built up in peace.

The Government agreed that methods employed by individual recruiters were in some cases unsatisfactory and that they were to blame for making promises which they knew to be untrue. As regards European officers, the rules about learning the language would again be strictly enforced. Furthermore, officers would be encouraged by all means to acquire full knowledge of their men not only in the Service but in their homes. This was a rather obvious reference to officers such as Commander King whom the report criticised. It stated that he did not impress the Commission as a reliable witness and was "an unfortunate choice for command of the *Talwar*. The incidents which had occurred were the occasion rather than the cause of the mutiny." The report repeated the allegations of *Talwar* ratings that he had called them "sons of coolies and bitches" when reprimanding them for not showing proper marks of respect and obeying his instructions.

The Government's belief that officers should acquire "full knowledge of their men not only in the Service but also in their homes" was extremely important. Failure of the European officers to do so led the Indian ratings, rightly or wrongly, to believe that their officers, lacking sympathy and understanding, regarded them (the ratings) as inferior beings who deserved to be discriminated against because in any case "they knew no better". Injudicious remarks such as "these men were swinging on trees before we came to their country and civilised them" heard in naval messes were hardly pleasing to the Indian stewards who served the officers! Ignorance of and disrespect for the ancient culture and civilisation of India was regarded as an added humiliation by the sensitive ratings.

The Government expressed its determination to do everything possible to eliminate any suspicion of racial discrimination; to have Indian officers posted to the command of ships and to the posts of Executive Officers of ships, and to higher staff appointments as they acquired sufficient seniority and experience.

It must be remembered that at the time the Government expressed such views, India was not yet independent and there was no guarantee that it would be so in the near future. Hence its conclusions were framed in a rather tentative manner.

Questions of pay, allowances and pensions and other conditions of Service would be examined by the Post-War Pay Commission, an inter-Services body of the Department of Defence. Regarding canteens, naval canteens were to be improved. The important point of promotion to commissioned ranks from the lower deck would receive high priority. This, it was felt, would serve as an added incentive to efficiency for the ratings, apart from democratising the Service and making for a better spirit of comradeship between all ranks.

The view was expressed by the Government that the mutiny was not organised by an outside agency though politics and political influence had a very great effect. That the mutiny was "not organised by an outside agency" may be, I think, open to question. If there were not sufficient evidence to incriminate an outside body as such, the earlier entry into the Service of nationalist-minded ratings, attracted by suave promises of good pay and good living conditions, could not be ruled out as impossible. During the War, conditions in India were becoming increasingly difficult with food shortages and rising prices, and the comparative security offered by the Armed Forces in this respect proved an alluring bait. Moreover, such ratings would not easily sever their connections with politicians and nationalists who were expected to become useful at some future moment. These political affiliations were doubtless made use of when thoughts of mutiny were in the air, as was perhaps natural in the prevailing circumstances.

The leading Congress figures might well have disavowed the mutiny, but the lower ranks and the civilians generally had evinced tremendous sympathy for the cause of the ratings precisely because it appeared to be bound up with the political situation. In this tie-up, Mahatma Gandhi himself could scarcely refrain from referring simultaneously to the mutiny and the critical political conditions.

In a statement on February 24, 1946, shortly after the mutiny ended, he said:

> In resorting to mutiny, the Royal Indian Navy ratings were badly advised. If it was for a grievance, fancied or real, they should have waited for the guidance and intervention of the political leaders of their choice. If they mutinied for the freedom of India they were doubly wrong. They could not do so without a call from a prepared revolutionary party. They were thoughtless in believing that by their might they would deliver India from foreign domination.
>
> Are the three Cabinet Ministers coming to deceive a great nation? It is neither manly nor womanly to think so. What would be lost by waiting? The nation will gain by trusting. The deceiver loses when there is a correct response from the deceived.
>
> The problem is knotty, probably the knottiest that has ever confronted a statesman. It is possible that the mission will put forth an insoluble conundrum. So much the worse for them. If they are intent on finding an honest way out of the difficulties of their own creation, I have no doubt there is a way, but the nation, too, has to play the game. If it does, the barricades must be left aside, at least for the time being.

Characteristically, Mahatma Gandhi deplored violence of any sort and stated his views in no uncertain terms. Furthermore, consistent with his teaching of truth and non-violence, he exhorted his followers to leave every door open to negotiation and treat their opponents with all fairness in the hope that they would react favourably and constructively—which in this all-important crisis they did. This had subsequent far-reaching and beneficial consequences, culminating in India's continued membership of the Commonwealth of Nations, notwith-standing decades of struggle. But more of this later.

Meanwhile, Pandit Nehru who was in the midst of his Bihar electioneering campaign at the outbreak of the mutiny, cancelled it and on his arrival at Allahabad said, "I am greatly worried by the Bombay situation.[1] I feel that by going there I might be of some help."

At Bombay, he was met by Sardar Vallabhai Patel who accompanied him on a tour of inspection of the devastated areas of the city. Nehru and Patel also saw victims of the civil disturbances who were seriously injured and taken to hospitals in all parts of the city.

Speaking later, Mr Nehru sharply criticised the counter-revolution-aries (including the communists) who had "led the people of Bombay into bloody rioting". He further declared:

> If a revolution becomes necessary, India's leaders would give the signal. Unsocial elements have exploited the credulity of inno-cent people.
>
> We have all the virtues for winning our freedom, but we lack the discipline which is essential for a free country. During the last four days, many things have happened in this city which are bad. Many other things also happened which are good.

Turning to the visit of the Cabinet delegation, Mr Nehru said:

> There are fair chances of some agreement, based on inde-pendence emerging from the talks that are to begin on the arrival of the British Cabinet's delegation. Even if the chances are less, it is the right policy for us to work for such an agreement provided always that we stick to our anchor. . . . In the final analysis Britain's interest lay with the salving of some goodwill as well as of other things in India, by co-operating in the attainment of India's independence rather than by being forced to recognise it some years later and lose everything.

Referring to the Indian naval mutiny, Pandit Nehru demanded a public trial for which, he said, the Congress party would organise the defence of those involved . . . it was folly to put up inferior violence to oppose the superior violence at the disposal of the authorities. Speak-ing of the recent sentences of imprisonment for cruelty on two Indian

---

1. In a statement in the House of Lords, Lord Pethwick-Lawrence listed the following casualties and damage in Bombay: 223 persons killed; 1,037 persons injured; looting and destruction of 9 banks, 32 government grain shops (which the public could ill afford to lose in the prevailing famine), 30 other shops, 10 post offices and 10 police stations.

army officers who joined the INA, Nehru contended that cruelty had to be considered in its context and in the present situation it was surely unwise to pass these theoretical sentences which would later be rescinded.

> . . . there is a desire and a strong urge on both sides to come to a peaceful settlement and it may well be that success will come to us. Britain should not forget that today she is addressing a sensitive, proud and virile people who will not put up with any patronage or anything smacking of superiority.

Following the lead given by Gandhi and Nehru, the nationalist *Bombay Chronicle* commented editorially:

> [These] events were most lamentable and unprecedented since the Indian Mutiny of 1857.

Taking a somewhat different position, the nationalist and leftist *Free Press Journal* of Bombay, stated:

> A strike in which the present one has occurred is more than a strike. It is part of the national feeling for freedom and it has to be judged as such.

At the start of the mutiny the *Manchester Guardian* succintly summarised the position:

> . . . To the frustration of waiting for release from discipline after the War is over, which we have experienced in our own forces [it was reported that two million BORs had been demobilised by then] there have been added for these Indian ratings passions and prejudices, easily stirred to flame which rise naturally from this tense moment in their country's history. We cannot wonder that this mutiny and its reaction should also excite the civilian population.

Extreme left-wing and communist groups in France were reported to have reacted "with instinctive sympathy to colonial rioters and mutineers while at the same time feeling sorry (!) for a British lion whose teeth and claws are too worn in all these struggles, and whose purse is too empty to deal with this situation".

While the French communists used the troubles confronting Britain in India and in Egypt as propaganda against Britain, the right-wing in France urged popular support and sympathy for Britain as "the fate of both French and British empires were linked together."

In Moscow's *Pravda*, the Indian naval mutiny and the accompanying riots were fully reported together with reference to an election speech in which a Congress party leader had proclaimed "a final and decisive battle with Britain". Yet, typically no reference was made to the Congress', and in particular to Gandhi's, denunciation of the outbreaks of violence or to the prospective and widely approved visit to India of the three British Cabinet Ministers. Egypt, Persia, Palestine and Indonesia were also dealt with by *Pravda* on similar lines.

This theme was later pursued by Moscow Radio with its characteristic vigour in subverting other nationalisms for its own ends. The Indian people, it said, wanted a new way of life, "but are coming into conflict with stubborn attempts to turn everything back into the old channel". It was the same in Egypt; the people felt that Britain desired "to carry on its old policy of occupation, with no wish to satisfy Egypt's demands for national independence". The average man everywhere (including Russia, surely!) was wondering why the great documents drawn up during the War were not applied. "Deeds don't live up to words: promises made during the War are not being kept . . . The colonial powers are still seeking to keep the subject peoples under the old intolerable regime."

It should be noted that not long after, Churchill had occasion to make his famous speech at Fulton, USA where he spoke of Russia's "Iron Curtain across Europe".

It was believed then that the Soviet Union's criticisms against Britain were due to the Soviet peoples having to face enormous tasks of reconstruction, and needing a strengthened sense of confidence stemming from the belief that the Soviet Union was the only stable country in a world of change!

With Gandhian moral principles wedded to the ideas of modern nationalism as the background of the organisation of the Congress, and through it, of the freedom struggle, added poignancy attaches to the concluding words of the Nehru Interim Government's comment on the report:

> It seems to us that but for the mistakes made, this great catastrophe might never have happened—a catastrophe which caused so much damage, suffering and bloodshed, and which has left so much unhappiness and bitterness in this Service.

A constant refrain running through the speeches of Gandhi, Nehru, Patel and other Congress leaders right through the years was insistence on discipline. For they felt, and rightly, that without discipline the revolution, unique in its characteristic of functioning lawfully at certain periods and clandestinely at others, would end in disaster. But for this iron discipline, the Congress would never have become the powerful organisation it turned out to be. Members of the Congress were expected to exercise the greatest self-control and obedience to the decisions of the Working Committee – its supreme governing body – only *after* these were arrived at as a result of full consultations and nearly unanimous consent.

Towering over all other Congress leaders was the personality of Gandhi, who was once described as a "unique Indian dictator who ruled by love". His authority was final, his word was law—but only after he had *won over* the considerable opposition to his authority sometimes forcefully expressed by his nearest followers, including Nehru. Thus no law is so well obeyed as that which is voluntarily and happily self-imposed! A law inspired by love and consent freely obtained is guaranteed successful acceptance. This was the fundamental principle on which Gandhi and his followers constantly sought to operate. The doctrine of truth and non-violence evoked greater moral courage, self-sacrifice and self-restraint in suppressing a natural and instinctive reaction to hit out violently when attacked. It was *not* non-resistance. It was the utmost resistance put up in a non-violent manner. It eschewed hatred of one's opponent and enjoined respect for him or her. Accordingly, no hatred was felt for the British people as such but only for the *system* of foreign rule. Similar resistance would have been offered to the regime of any other colonial power if it had ruled India. Gandhi translated into action the prophetic injunction of "hate the sin and not the sinner".

Thus, with the prospect of the transfer of sovereign power and the entire governmental apparatus, the reason for hostility and bitterness would disappear, to be replaced by cooperation and goodwill.

10

Postscript

The stirring events of February 1946 left an indelible impression on those who witnessed their occurrence at the time. But fifty years later they need to be placed in perspective. As observed in the Preface, the world was in turmoil after the Second World War, and India was no exception.

At the outbreak of the War in 1939 it was necessary to put the Navy on a war footing geared to contribute to India's war effort. The Navy had come a long way since its early beginnings as the Bombay Marine, then as the Royal Indian Marine and in 1934 as the Royal Indian Navy. Under British rule the nucleus had been created and the foundation laid for the subsequent Indian Navy, as it was called in January 1950, when India became a Republic, the first to achieve such a status in the British Commonwealth of Nations (when the term 'British' was dropped).

The role of the Indian Navy today is to protect the country's territorial waters and maritime interests. India's coastline stretches for 7500 km and even more when the Andaman and Nicobar islands in the Bay of Bengal are taken into account. Since the adoption of the United Nations Law of the Sea Convention in 1992, the country has gained added responsibility including known oil reserves in the Arabian Sea, a large fishing fleet and a number of important ports. Their importance will increase as the Indian economy expands and demands for energy, food and trade will grow as well.

Modernising the Indian Navy is thus a matter of necessity and not just one of muscle-flexing. While in 1995 the Navy received a large increase in funds, India's Defence Budget has decreased so much since the end of the Cold War in the late eighties that, according to a recent report by the Institute for Defence Studies and Analysis, it ranks twenty-fifth out of thirty-seven Asian nations. The procurement budget, a measure of how much the country actually spends on weapons, has generally followed this trend. Nevertheless, the increase in Navy funds reflects the growing importance of the Indian Ocean in Delhi's strategic calculations.

To appreciate the progress in the role of the Navy it is necessary to recall the period after Independence and the spirit which animated its personnel. The last British admiral in command of the Navy handed over charge to his Indian successor over ten years later, in April 1958. In a message to the Navy, Admiral R.P. Katari, who succeeded Sir Stephen Carlill as Chief of Naval Staff, said his appointment was less significant for his personal success than for the fact that it denoted the progress made by the Navy since Independence. The Navy had many more milestones to pass before it could become fully efficient. He was sure that he could fully rely on the officers and men of the Navy to make the Service the finest defence organisation in the country, and of which it could be proud.

In his farewell message to the Indian Navy, Admiral Carlill said:

> At sunset today(April 22) the Flag of the last British Chief of Staff will be hauled down and an era in the annals of the Navy will come to an end. It is exactly thirty-three months ago today that I had the honour of becoming your Chief of Naval Staff and they have been months of great pride and happiness to me. Whatever I have been able to do has been amply repaid by your own enthusiasm and support, which have been a source of inspiration to me and for which I am deeply grateful. I leave with unshake-able confidence in your future and with the certain knowledge that under the inspiring leadership of Admiral Katari you will go on from strength to strength and prove yourselves worthy of your great country.

After Admiral Carlill paid a courtesy call on the President, Dr Rajendra Prasad, he attended a farewell reception at which Defence Minister at the time, Mr Krishna Menon, and Army and Air Force Chiefs were present.

The continued use of British methods of training and organisation in all branches of the Navy indicated the degree of cooperation between British and Indian navies. The men of the Indian Navy came from all parts of India and although they were of different faiths and belonged to different castes and cultures, they worked as a team. One of the fields in which the Navy proved very useful was its role in carrying India's message of goodwill and friendship to other countries in Europe, Africa, East and West Asia.

For instance, an Indian Navy ship visited Israel shortly after the assassination of its Prime Minister, Itzhak Rabin, on November 4, 1995 and this was in keeping with the unique measure of sympathy and support displayed by the Indian Government on that sad occasion, when it declared a day of state mourning and cancelled all its activities and functions in India and abroad, a gesture much appreciated by Israel's people as reported in their media. Later in November a goodwill visit was paid to China.

After partition in 1947, India's small Navy was considerably reduced, as roughly one-third of it went to Pakistan together with three of its important naval establishments. So in developing her Navy, India had to begin almost from scratch including dealing with problems of modernising armaments and equipment and the gradual 'Indianisation' of the Service.

Destroyers, frigates and coastal minesweepers had to be purchased or renovated. British cruisers were adapted for use by the Indian Navy and, in the sphere of naval training and maintenance of shore establishments, the achievement of complete self-sufficiency was the aim. This is still the aim as Admiral V.S. Shekhawat, Chief of Naval Staff until September 1996, stated in New Delhi that "a navy has to be built and cannot be bought" (The Times of India, November 24, 1995).[1]

Among the significant projects recently approved for the Navy is the construction of India's largest naval base at Karwar near Goa. The base will take about twenty-five years to build, and the first phase, about ten years, will cost about Rs 1300 crore. Indigenously-built warships currently in hand include three Delhi-class destroyers which will enter service from 1997, three Godavari-class frigates, four

---

1. The admiral, in his farewell address, urged the Indian Government to increase its annual allocation to the Navy's budget, and exercise foresight in assessing its future requirements.